Praise for *Your Favori*

"Leigh Chadwick is an absurdist with a heart of gold, funny and strange on the page and always precisely herself, no matter the persona she's taking on—including that of *Your Favorite Poet*. These poems are a party come to break your heart, wondrously smart and wonderfully weird."

—Matt Bell, author of *Appleseed*

"Leigh Chadwick is a sui generis writer who captures, with searing clarity, the luridness of our present moment of pop culture obsession and bullet ridden schools. Leigh's poems do more than provoke, they invite the reader into moments of tenderness and hope that give us a reason to cling to this beautiful and awful world. Chadwick has her finger squarely on the pulse of the contemporary moment, and her poems are funny, joyous, and sad. In short, they are a wonder."

—Andrew Bertaina, author of *One Person Away From You*

"From the very beginning, starting with the prologue, Leigh Chadwick wastes neither time nor words. She writes with an honesty and longing that chronicles what it is to be alive in such violent, unstable times—what it is to be a mother when nothing is certain. Her words offer hope and yet brutal honesty, and we must decide how to hold both at once inside each breath of her poetry."

—Adrienne Marie Barrios, editor-in-chief of *Reservoir Road Literary Review*

"From suburban heart-sprawl to bacterial conjunctivitis to onions in the attic, Leigh Chadwick brings tears to the eyes. Mixing dubstep and dada, wit and luscious images, these poems are voice-driven kazoos in a church pew during communion. If Chadwick isn't your favorite poet, she may be your favorite poem."

—Alina Stefanescu, author of *Dor*

"Somehow I get the feeling that since Leigh Chadwick is here to write about our world that everything will be all right."

—Maureen Seaton, author of *Undersea*

"Reading Leigh Chadwick, I get the sense that there are many Leigh Chadwicks out there—which is a pretty comforting thought to me. Or maybe reading Leigh Chadwick gives me the sense that there are infinite versions of ourselves—each striving for perplexing and imperfect grace? In any case, it is comforting that we have this one Leigh Chadwick, the serious and hilarious writer who has filled her singular collection of poetry, *Your Favorite Poet*, with as much righteous indignation, feral silliness, and profound joy as a single version of any of us can take."

—Shane Kowalski, author of *Small Moods*

Your Favorite Poet
Leigh Chadwick

Hardcover ISBN: 9781087943428
Paperback ISBN: 9781088068519
Ebook ISBN: 9781087943640
Ebook also available at publisher's website, malarkeybooks.com

Cover design by Angelo Maneage
Typesetting by Alan Good

First paperback edition, published in September 2022 by Malarkey Books. Pretty much identical to the hardcover except for this part and where we added a little notice at the end about Leigh Chadwick's next book, *Sophomore Slump*, out in May 2023.

For A & L—my two favorite hearts

Table of Contents

15. Prologue

22

19. The First Poem in *Your Favorite Poet*, a Collection of Poetry
    Written by Leigh Chadwick and Published by Malarkey
    Books in July of 2022
20. Deer Poem
21. Every Day a Ghost Town Loses a Map
22. Cough Medicine Works Best When You Drink It
    Straight from the Bottle
23. Frankie Cosmos Is a Good Band Name
24. Inspired by Actual Events
25. Bullets Not Included
26. I Want to Tell Your Bacteria to Stop It
    with the Conjunctions
27. Suburbs
28. I Saw Jesus in a Minivan
29. The World Is a Wilt
30. Coheed and Cambria Is My Favorite Font
31. The Domesticity of Spoiled Milk
32. How I Learned to Stop Drinking Starbucks and Wait
    Patiently for My Parents to Die So I Can Cash in on My
    Inheritance
33. This Is the Fifteenth Poem
34. What Do People Do When People Do People Things?
35. I'm Good with Purgatory, How Are You?

36. If I Don't Die First, I Will Know She's Dead
      and Then What Is There Left to Do but Also Be Dead
37. Pimento
38. Thursday
39. I Build a Time Machine and Push Samuel Colt
      Off a Cliff
40. A Map to Heaven
41. I Delete Every Emotion That Was Never
      Worth Capitalizing
42. Sunday School
43. The Third Strokes Album Is Only Good if You
      Don't Play It
44. Regarding the Sheets We Bought at the Store
      That Sells Sheets
45. What Cheer
46. A Mass of Thoughts
47. Cover Band
48. I Still Like That Movie Where Nicolas Cage
      Plays Nicolas Cage
50. Poem Written on the Notes App on My iPhone While Sitting
      on the Couch Watching Sesame Street with My Daughter
51. Dinosaur Poem Written in June
52. Deleted Scenes from *Friday Night Lights*
53. Basketball Twitter Is a Dumpster Fire
54. Chris Paul Calls Jake from State Farm but He Doesn't Answer
56. Donner Parties in the Mountains

Foreplay

59. I.
60. II.
61. III.
62. IV.
63. V.
64. VI.
65. VII.
66. VIII.
67. IX.
68. X.

71. Bump in the Night
72. Day 219
73. Sloths
74. How to Spend Your First Week Being Furloughed from
    Work
76. Jesus Auditions to Play Jesus
78. Shade
79. Lesson Plan
80. Hint of Color
81. Hospital Poem
82. Somewhere in the Middle We Will Fuck Up
83. I Think Tumbleweed
84. How to Make Water
85. How to Be a Poet Days After Finding Out
    Your Husband Cheated on You
86. How to Make It to One Day, Five Years Later
87. You
88. The Poem of Tiny Clouds
89. How to Bruise a City
90. Volcano Poem
91. Daughters of the State
92. Department of Children Services
93. A Library of Limbs

Brief Excerpts from Leigh Chadwick Is Your Favorite Poet: An Unauthorized Biography, Written and Edited by Leigh Chadwick

97. I.
98. II.
99. III.
100. IV.
101. V.
102. VI.
104. VII.
105. VIII.
107. IX.
108. X.
109. XI.
110. XII.
111. XIII.

Epilogue

114. The Questionnaire of Good Intentions
116. That One Week in Cedar Rapids, Iowa
117. Based on a True Story
118. Chocolate Chip Pancakes
119. Utah Is a Documentary
120. The Study of Sky
121. One Times Nine
122. Pudding Poem
123. Molt
124. Every Year Is a Year

Acknowledgments
Thank You
About the Author

Your Favorite Poet

Prologue

I write a book of poems. I title it *Your Favorite Poet*. It is a good book of poems. To celebrate writing a good book of poems, I tape origami wings to my shoulder blades and drink a bottle of red grapes as I unfold an atlas and promise to find you, so I can tell you that I wrote a book of poems titled *Your Favorite Poet* and that the book is good and that you are the reason these words were born, that they were given these pages, and then I am searching for you, searching in caves and on top of mountains— above the trees or in the trees or sometimes both—and I sleep in deserted bears and with my feet buried beneath the sand in Naples, and that one night in Lima, where I briefly lose my heart in a missionary's broken condom. And then after months of teaching cursive to angels in the snow and tracing my fingertips along the atlas, now tattered and ripped and itself lost, there you are, in a bed made of smaller beds, and your eyes are full of sleep and your breath is tinted julep and after climbing on top of you, you say, *There you are,* and I say, *I wrote a book of poems and it is good and you are in it and yes, here I am,* and you say nothing because everything is already said because these pages are already written and you are real enough that I can pretend that I can be the same.

22

The First Poem in *Your Favorite Poet*, a Collection of Poetry Written by Leigh Chadwick and Published by Malarkey Books in July of 2022

The road to heaven is lined with bullet casings and leftover pieces of children too slow to duck. The air smells like thoughts and prayers. Above the road lined with bullet casings but below heaven, the sky has the sniffles. The birds sneeze. The clouds cough. I fill a Super Soaker with NyQuil and point it at the sky. Someone sticks an exclamation mark between each of my ribs. I don't know why. I don't ask. Instead, I count to ten thoughts and prayers and wonder who is caring for the pipe bombs hiding in the boy's garage. I worry for every unlocked door. I close my eyes. I don't have to wait for the flash.

Deer Poem

The first time I saw you, you were a deer grazing in the field behind
my house. It was morning, early enough for the dew to still be settled.
I was standing in the living room, looking out the window as I watched
you, your head down, teeth pressed against the earth. I thought *milk
thistle* but didn't know why. I wished you to stay. I blinked, and you
were still there. I did a load of laundry, and you were still there. I
painted the kitchen lagoon. Again, you were still there. I waited for
the sky to cry. The sky never cried, but you stayed, unmoved, your
mouth still pressed against the earth, the grass nothing but dirt. The
sun began to fall. I opened my back door and walked out into the field.
Your ears twitched. Your antlers grew smaller antlers. Your heart
threatened nothing but its next beat.

Every Day a Ghost Town Loses a Map

I wake up with an entire town planted in my heart. No one comes to the town that was planted in my heart, and by my second cup of coffee, the town has become a ghost town. For breakfast, I butter my toast and cough spirits already dead. I charm the tumbleweeds as they roll through my lungs. I need to trim my fingernails, but August is my least favorite grave. No matter the decorations inside my medicine cabinet, I am always too tired to bundle winter. Somewhere in my abdomen is where you can find my dream of fidelity. *Ignore the wild horses eating themselves*, I tell you as the ghost doctor in the ghost town hands me a glass and says, *Go ahead and drink, I dare you. You can call it beer, but it is sand. You can call it water, but it is sand.* In the ghost town, a mile south of the general store, a row of tombstones reads *Ghosts are just angels too ugly to touch the sky*. I drink from the glass the ghost doctor gave me. *All of it*, he says. *Everything here is me and everything here is sand.* With the glass still pressed against my lips, I think, *Even the sand is sand*. I finish everything in the glass, and then I eat the glass. I cough a dust bowl and begin to spin in circles until I turn into a tornado, gathering every grain of sand and what was built on the grains of sand—all that can never be forgotten.

Cough Medicine Works Best When You Drink It Straight from the Bottle

It is the year of baking bread. Of mouths tinted blue. Of *this is worse than it should have been.* It's Saturday. I no longer believe in trees. The breeze smells like its own sequel. I sell the film rights to my left thigh. I self-publish the middle of the Atlantic. I ask Tennessee, *Do you regret being Tennessee?* Does anyone remember dial tones or the dream about the wolf who ate the other wolves? I get a letter in the mail stating that the warranty on my soul is about to expire. I haven't left the house since the last time I left the house. I used to believe in so many things: hospital waiting rooms, soap that smelled like stardust, the monotony of an afternoon of chewing on leftover ice from my glass of iced coffee. The speed limit in heaven is tachycardia per hour. How far down a throat can a tube go? I am [redacted] but not [redacted]. Someone locked the front door. The past is nothing but dried burgundy, or maybe it's a lake or possibly a river if you're bold enough to call it that.

Frankie Cosmos Is a Good Band Name

I always wait at least forty-five minutes after therapy before having sex. Every spring I pick up a second job planting pollen in dandelions. On Thursdays I listen to the same Frankie Cosmos track on repeat as I follow myself into the afternoon. Most mornings I wake up in a bed full of smaller beds. This morning is one of those mornings. You are next to me. Light trips through the blinds. *Leigh*, you say. *You*, I say. You ask if I knew I was sleeping while I was sleeping. I don't answer. My eyes are too busy tracing your lips, the morning of your mouth. You say my name again, followed by something about a bagel. I think about my name. *Leigh. Leigh. Leigh. Leigh.* I like the way it slips out of your throat, as if it's coated in margarine.

Inspired by Actual Events

My sadness drinks ink by the stanza, chews on pen caps, paints the walls silverfish. It ties the earth around my neck as I feed syllables to the birds. My sadness coughs sheep. It dips the clouds in gravy. I only buy eggplants when I'm drunk. I never pay extra for guacamole. I climbed a mountain so I could call and tell you I climbed a mountain, but I didn't read the Surgeon General's Warning on the side of the mountain, so I didn't know about the lack of cellphone reception or the thinning air sneaking out of the cracks in my ribs. Everything smells purple. It doesn't matter. My sadness beats a heart so crisp. I dream in lisps. I take five pills every morning to forget the definition of *feel*. I take the batteries out of my remote control and put them in my coffee. Could we not? The strawberries are ripe. The blossoms are here. I'm teaching my daughter how to cocoon. I put a picture of a milk carton on the side of a milk carton in case the milk carton gets lost. I don't know, how about you? There is lavender in my taste in the window-stained fog in the wrist of your lungs. How could anyone know the taste buds of a dead boy's tongue? Someone put onions in the attic and now the ceiling is crying.

Bullets Not Included

On Highway 61, a billboard reads: FREE BULLETS INCLUDED WITH THE PURCHASE OF ANY GUN. At Target, I buy my daughter a Fisher-Price electronic drum machine. The back of the box states: BATTERIES NOT INCLUDED. I look in every closet in Tennessee. I find bullets but no batteries. My daughter presses on her plastic drum machine and nothing happens. I drive past a pawn shop on Lincoln Street, directly across from the Head Start. I drive to the last Toys "R" Us that still hides the haunts of laughter in shredded caves of concrete. I carry my daughter through the rubble of abandoned Super Soakers and Slip 'N Slides. I sit her on a giraffe's neck. The giraffe coughs. We feed it a cough drop. We look up. I count fourteen clouds and think of Austin. My daughter points toward a hill covered in trees curled like semicolons. She asks, *What is this?* I tell her it's the amount of free bullets that are packaged in the backs of semis rolling down I-75. At home, I make chocolate chip pancakes for dinner. I still haven't bought batteries for my daughter's drum machine. In Alabama, an employee working for a company that distributes water goes to work and shoots and shoots and shoots. I wonder if his bullets were free. I wonder why it's harder to buy batteries than bullets. I wonder when bullets will get tired of running into people. I wonder if you put two bullets in a remote control, will CNN report another shooting in a warehouse? I am trying to figure out why some people get to exist and others don't. I should buy batteries. I should be a better mother. Four mass shootings in six hours, thirty-eight wounded, six dead. Everywhere is scary when there are more bullets than batteries. When there are more guns than song.

I Want to Tell Your Bacteria
to Stop It with the Conjunctions

My daughter has bacterial conjunctivitis. Her eyes have turned into a river filled with bodies meant to be forgotten. I take my daughter to the doctor. The doctor checks my daughter's eyes for alligators, but the doctor only finds tadpoles. The doctor plucks the tadpoles out of her eyes with tweezers. She puts the tadpoles in a Ziploc baggie and gives the baggie to my daughter. When we get home, the tadpoles have turned into tiny frogs. My daughter punches holes in the top of a Mason jar, fills the jar with a lake and drops the frogs in the jar. She names all of the frogs Darwin. She takes her Mason jar full of Darwins to her kindergarten class's show and tell, where she stands in front of the class and holds the Mason jar above her head. The kids watch the tiny frogs swim in circles. The kids watch them drink Budweiser and then drunkenly leap over each other. My daughter blinks and every science fiction movie becomes a true story. The kids watch the frogs evolve into monkeys and the Mason jar turn into a barrel. My daughter sneezes and a tornado breaks Oklahoma in half. Moments later and now the monkeys are humans. The barrel, a Motel 6. My daughter coughs and the San Andreas fault ruptures. The teacher cracks his knuckles, and an AR-15 invites a grocery store over for dinner. In my daughter's hands, the humans are still humans, but the Motel 6 is now a nursing home. Next to the nursing home sits a mortuary, overlooking the river draining from my daughter's eyes.

Suburbs

It's a chore to crawl through hidden tunnels
just to find a taste of medicine. I have taken to eating nicotine patches
and remote controls. You, all chest and song.
You, the left side of the bed. I have killed so many of my darlings
my trashcan is overflowing. The sink is clogged.
My arms ache. I fall asleep in the corner of a hotel bar.
My dreams come with a receipt, but I never have the energy
to return them. I hold a press conference to announce
my retirement from drinking through a straw.
There isn't a song in the world I want to listen to right now.
My fingernails caked in soil, growing weeds
after each shower. I have become something so quiet.
I wake up nothing but the hand on my lower back, the pillow
on my other pillow. I have never met a good intention
that hasn't slipped on a patch of ice.
The Surgeon General's Warning on the inside of my bottom lip
reads *If you* _____ *(noun)* _____ *(emoji)* _____ *(proper noun),*
you will turn into a mausoleum. You, the kindling
in my hands. You, a pulse. A thirst. My muted lust. You,
the *oh* and the *how* and the *want*, this desire for touch,
to be agreed that I am worth, to be a deer running into headlights,
to be mood, everything and all, to tell you, *I am waiting*
to be found in the smallest crater on the moon.

I Saw Jesus in a Minivan

I saw Jesus in a minivan. I think it was a Dodge. We were idled next to each other at a red light. Jesus was sitting in the driver's seat, a cherry slushie in his left hand, the straw pressed between his lips. The windows of the minivan were cracked. He was listening to "Psycho Killer" by the Talking Heads. I listened to him listen to "Psycho Killer" by the Talking Heads. I wanted to follow him to wherever he was going, see if I could buy him a beer. I wanted to sit in the back booth of a bar and ask him if he knew who smoked the last clove cigarette. If he had a favorite ocean. If the Dead Sea was always supposed to be called that. If stairs were created so hips would have an excuse to break. If he ever swallowed mistletoes in the basement of a brothel. I needed to know if he knew what the river hides. From the minivan, David Byrne was singing *Psycho Killer/Qu'est-ce que c'est*. The light turned green. A quarter mile down the road, the concrete rippled. Neither of us moved.

The World Is a Wilt

I've decided to prepare for the end of the world, so I spend the afternoon packing a survival kit. On the front of the survival kit, I write *Do not open. Beware, wild snakes.* I don't know why I wrote *wild snakes,* since domestic snakes are just as scary, so I cross out *wild* and scribble *BIG* over it. I pack the survival kit with a week's worth of weather. I pack it with my calcified heart, the third aisle of Costco, the night we melted the duvet. I pack my Submittable password, the submission fee to *Narrative,* the chapbook my daughter promised to write when she learns how to write. I take a break from packing and fill my coffee maker with fresh grounds of hazel. I eat a bluebird. Outside, it's June. I go for a walk. The trees remind me that the color green still exists. I pick up a tree and put it in my back pocket. When I get home, I pack the tree in my survival kit. I have enough room in the kit for one more thing. I decide to pack the memory of our third date: the picnic at the lake, the loaf of bread, the ducks, your body pressed against my sundress as my thighs turned sunset.

Coheed and Cambria Is My Favorite Font

Today is a Monday full of typos. I keep waking up in a sea of lions. A head swarming with bees. A mouthful of bears. I've never tried laughing underwater and I never will. This is the third poem where the ghost of my grandmother tells me to chew with my mouth closed. I tell my therapist, *Taylor Swift is still in love and that's all the hope I need for now.* It's been so long since I've said hello to the woods, I don't even know if they're still making trees. For foreplay, I watch my husband swallow all of the bullets in the world. He unloads the dishwasher while I press my ear against the refrigerator and listen to it quietly hum. When I close my eyes, I still see the blood from the kids on the other kids' shoes. Imagine if bullets made people bleed in Comic Sans. I like the song that goes, *Who gives a fuck about the* Oxford American? I buy a round of bullets but forget to buy the gun that goes with them. I ask Siri, *What happens if you put a bullet in the microwave?* Siri says, *The same thing that happens when the feathers in your pillow fly away.* On TV, CNN is reporting that the CDC says we should ban assault rifles, and that, even if you're fully vaccinated, if you fall off a cliff, you're probably still going to die.

The Domesticity of Spoiled Milk

—After Ben Niespodziany

I google *autofiction* and immediately lose my virginity for a third time. I mail a forest to the moon and the moon says, *What the fuck am I going to do with a forest?* The moon mails the forest back. By the time the forest shows up in my mailbox, it is dead or almost dead, so I put the forest in hospice. I hire a river to fuck up a bunch of matches. I quit poetry to start a chillwave band with Ben. We open for Wavves in an empty parking lot a few states away from the Pitchfork Music Festival. After, we set out on a solo tour of the East Coast, playing behind tiny desks in the backs of Office Depots. When I get home from tour, you tell me you quit love to wear socks with sandals. I take off my skin and run it through the dishwasher. Ben quits the band to open a library for books that never learned how to read. You open a Hanes Outlet in the closet. I find a snake in the sink, its belly bloated, full of air from the last ghost ever named Fred.

How I Learned to Stop Drinking Starbucks and Wait Patiently for My Parents to Die so I Can Cash in on My Inheritance

I put another avocado in my safety deposit box. I sell my plasma and save half the cookie the nurse gives me for breakfast the next morning. I am poor and so are you and if you're not poor then who did you kill? My loans have loans. My bank account coughs dust. My daughter is growing up to be a history lesson in debt. I own a house and I don't know why. Soon, I will not own a house and I will know exactly why. I've never eaten avocado toast, but I drink milk without the lactose, and it's like forty-two cents more a gallon than regular milk. I type *stock market* into Google Maps. It takes me to a set of train tracks. I park my car in the middle of the tracks, turn off the engine, and wait.

This Is the Fifteenth Poem

I fly too close to the sun and then I am the sun.
I start a cover band that covers cover bands.
Does anyone still do the Wobble?
I skip ponds across pebbles as I ask you to ask me
which of the sounds you misheard as we kissed
in the forest. I'm growing melodies
in my scratch-and-sniff novel about the gift shop
that sells smaller gift shops.
Sixty-two of my feelings begin with a gun
going gun. If I were asked to write a review
of God, I wouldn't. Every lobotomy is half off
if you only pay for half of a lobotomy.
This is the fifteenth poem in my book full of poems.
The first fourteen poems in my book full of poems
are better, but you have to admit this one
is still pretty fucking good.

What Do People Do
When People Do People Things?

The sun, a crisp edge above the horizon, slowly stretches and yawns into morning. On the back patio, half a dozen cigarette butts in the ashtray. In the kitchen, a pot of coffee brews. Morning touches our bed in the simplest ways. Light against the blinds, the dim of day on my dimples, so pronounced you tell me, looking at them feels like someone is hollering from the other room. What is it about silence and night that makes daylight feel like dessert? A light moan. The rustle of sheets. Waking up to the smell of bacon. Somehow, the comforter got covered in tree sap, but we don't complain. Right now is what I miss most about right now. You tell me, *When I die, I want every sound to growl.* I don't say anything. Instead, I wipe the hazel from your upper lip. I kiss the tip of your chin. It's so sharp I worry I might slice myself in half.

I'm Good with Purgatory, How Are You?

A wolf dressed as a wolf. A boy the same. Fog bellyflops
on the concrete, backstrokes through the brush,
and now Highway 61 is eighty percent dead deer.
I missed my therapy appointment's therapy appointment,
and now my fake memories are being taught as history lessons.
Imagine this line red, a quote from Jesus saying, *Everything was
once bone and if it wasn't bone then it should've been.*
On the last day of November, I wake up in last night's clothes,
sneezing Morse code. You are next to me, using your pillow
as a hospital helipad, while at a high school in Michigan,
four more teenagers fail anatomy. An analogy is left
on a chalkboard in an empty classroom: *prom dress is to
body bag as [redacted] is to* _____*[redacted].*
You say, *Wasn't this yesterday?* I say, *Every day
is yesterday when a mophead is stained pink.*
Our daughter is beginning to learn how to walk.
Outside, the sky is drinking cough syrup. I tell you
I'm quitting poetry to build mortuaries next to high schools.
You look at me. I look at you looking at me.
Our daughter takes three steps and falls headfirst on the rug.

If I Don't Die First, I Will Know She's Dead and Then What Is There Left to Do but Also Be Dead

—For A.

That's not a question. This is: I ask Siri, *How many bullets does it take to get to the center of a daughter's spine?* Siri says, *Just one, but what's the rush?* I buy my daughter a burial plot. I fill it with cement. I say, *Look, there's nowhere else to go.* I say, *Stay, the magnolias are about to bloom.* I say, *Stay, always stay.*

Pimento

I read somewhere that every fourteen minutes a bullet makes another body forget how to be a body, and that if you plant a bullet you will grow a republican. Everywhere, the ground is painted pimento. The Midwest digs up Charlton Heston's grave and pulls the bullets from his cold, dead mouth. Oranges in California rot. Atlanta chips its fingernails. Colorado graduates college with a degree in PTSD. A Wal-Mart in Texas coughs bullet holes. A strip mall in Arizona coughs bullet holes. A warehouse in Indianapolis sneezes. No one says bless you.

Thursday

[Redacted] in the chest. [Redacted] in the neck. [Redacted] in the chest, again. Left arm limp. Right arm, too. Two days later they're still picking pieces of him off the street. Thursday comes and with it, the memory of candles. [Redacted] upside down. Dressed in a closed casket. An unpaid bar tab. A field of ostriches digging bomb shelters. The death of Auto-Tune. A simile. The casualness of grief. Soon, worms. A mountain dripping spring.

I Build a Time Machine
and Push Samuel Colt Off a Cliff

Spoons are my second-favorite utensil. If you climb a fence, you will be at the top of a fence. The same goes for trees and boulders and the guy named Steve who tends bar next to the better bar in Des Moines. The calendar on my iPhone says it's either the end of the world or the first Tuesday in May. It is more likely that you will get shot in the face than fall in love. I'm not sure that's true, but science is taking a nap and the sink in the kitchen is clogged. I miss David Berman, but I miss Elliott Smith more. I can't remember where I was when I heard Pavement for the first time. It doesn't matter. I always turn the sound up when we kiss. I never forget my daughter but I'm always losing my keys, so I attach my keys to my daughter. I build a time machine and go back to 1836 and push Samuel Colt off a cliff. When I get back, I eat a bowl of banana pudding. I go online and adopt an elephant. It costs twelve dollars a month.

A Map to Heaven

If you find me drinking alone, it's because I am. It started with lead poisoning and led to lead bleeding, which led to lead killing. I hate that this is another gun poem. That I am writing this instead of kissing my husband under a streetlamp. That I am writing this instead of kissing my husband under a streetlamp across from the first streetlamp we kissed under. Life is a quiet landscape I keep forgetting to give myself. Everything is a struggle when the batteries in your remote control die. It started in Colorado and then kept going: Virginia, Connecticut, Colorado, Colorado, Colorado, Florida, Texas, Florida, Texas, California, and the sequels that followed. The state gun of Texas is all of them. The state motto of Florida is *We're sorry we're real.* The state flag of Colorado is a library of limbs. The state bird of Vermont is a moose dipped in syrup. The alternative title for this poem is "Never Trust an Unlocked Door."

I Delete Every Emotion
That Was Never Worth Capitalizing

I can't remember the last time we fucked to the silence of alliteration. Minutes turn to miles and miles turn to decades. In ten years, we will be ten years older. We've sharpened our teeth into knives. We, the teeth, chewing through insurance copays and the congestion on I-95. We, the second coming. We, the militia. We, raw and hidden from the wind. There are sutures where sutures were never meant to be. I delete every emotion that was never worth capitalizing. I hum "This Tornado Loves You" while you press me against the kitchen sink. The dog is howling but we can't hear him. Someone is shooting someone but we're not paying attention. I tell you your sweat smells like sweat. It's a good thing. You tell me you can't remember if you paid the electric bill. A river runs down my left thigh. *You probably paid it*, I say.

Sunday School

In the beginning, God removes Adam's left kidney and molds it into an AR-15. Eve wraps herself in a ribbon of Merlot. Later, in a field of poppies, Cain shoots Abel in the back of the head. Later later, Moses unloads a clip into the burning bush. The Bible says, *What now?* There is no response. God can't talk with a bullet lodged in his esophagus. If you walk into the Red Sea, it's nothing but stepping on skeletons and sipping seltzer. Put a couple beers in Jonah and he'll tell you all about what a .50 BMG can do to the stomach of a whale. I start a nonprofit to raise money to give elephants guns. Darwin shoots a platypus because he's sick of being a sticker on the back bumper of a rusted-out Toyota Tercel. Moses climbs down the mountain, carrying a tablet with *It is everyone's right to bear arms* etched across the front, and now the bears are like, *Shit, how are we supposed to crawl to the river to catch salmon without any arms?* You can make a gun with a 3D printer, but at least we don't have to worry about Taylor Swift living alone in New York City anymore. I wish I could've told Noah, *It's not worth it. Rest your hands.* I'm saving up to put down a deposit on a spaceship I will never learn how to fly. As hard as they tried, giant sloths couldn't outrun a bullet. Those fuckers never had a chance.

The Third Strokes Album Is Only Good
If You Don't Play It

I am the feeling of the river. I am the wilted D.A.R.E. t-shirt at the thrift store. I am walking home from school. I am the building full of holes. I am the first Strokes album and sometimes the second but never the third. I am building a bridge. I am walking over the bridge I built. I am two minutes away from being two minutes older. I am primrose. I am March 13th. I am swallowing every bullet in the world as I feed lozenges to the giraffe with a sore throat. I am the start button on the PlayStation controller. I am *Mom what's for dinner?* I am 3 a.m. I am the last spindlehorn. I am the semicolon between *before* and *after*. I am hijacking past participles. I am sorry. I am the easiest way to fall. I am giving this poem a two-star review on Goodreads. I am all mouth and tongue. I am missing. I am minutes from _____ (noun). I am what the river stole: bone and paste and a Buffalo nickel and more bone. I am something of a good time. I am driving through Sugar Ditch. I am eastern. I am sky. I am lark. I am *babe babe babe babe*. I am contractually obligated to dream. I am a part-time mother of words. I am a full-time mother of mothers. I am playing "Blister in the Sun" to my daughter for the first time. I am good morning. I am a Rilo Kiley cover band. I am [*redacted due to copyright laws*]. I am parked where we are always parked. I am with. I am slipping. I am paused. I am *oh never mind*. I am too in love to care. I am at the top of the parking garage. I am a long-distance phone call to the moon. I am a star that got lost trying to find its grave. I am a wall shedding its paint. I am sharpening my teeth into knives. I am *hello*. I am my own doppelgänger. I am *hello*, again. I am dancing in the street with wings.

Regarding the Sheets We Bought
at the Store That Sells Sheets

I change the sheets after each time we touch between them. My favorite hobby is watching you watch me get dressed for work. What I'm trying to say is that I'm always changing the sheets.

What Cheer

Find me in the bathroom stall at Powell's
shooting enjambment into my veins
as my prescription bottles stand in front of a banner
with *Mission Accomplished* scribbled across the front.
Days later my pills write me a letter stating they've unionized.
They use the word *strike*, like they're aiming a missile
at a hospital or pointing the tip of a drone at a school.
My pills are tired, I am told, overused, I am told.
They are demanding lower copays, PTO, a less toxic
work environment. My pills, I am told, need their own pills.
There is nothing to do but find something
to do, so I break up with my brain. I quit poetry
to write better poetry. I buy a new dress
and then return the dress. I carry an extra set of tears
in my purse. I write in my journal, *What day of the week
hasn't been a band?* and then rip the page
out of the journal and eat a package of peanuts
even though I'm allergic to bees. I spend the weekend
building a three-car garage in my stomach
so I can have a place to keep the key that opens
the last cellar door. A place to hide the scent
of bleach, to cover whoever is undressed first.
A place to hold my grandfather who has grown
too tired to remember how to spell his own name.
A place to pack away the parts of me that haven't bled
in months, and my fingernails—the shade
of the world between my lips.

A Mass of Thoughts

I go to bed a Jehovah's Witness. I dream Armageddon filing its taxes. I dream people climbing out of the dirt and dusting off their cellphones. I bathe in ampersands and wake up a Scientologist. I sit on a televised couch. I tell my husband, *Sit with me. Name me a crater. Give me the sun.* I say, *Call me sensible magic.* People are dying and it's not even tomorrow yet. There is too much gun in guns. It's 2021 and my t-shirt still reads *I'D RATHER BE AT THE FYRE FESTIVAL.* Every night I wake up with a mouthful of dirty bathwater. I hire myself to play myself sitting on a couch, watching a shot-for-shot remake of the shot-for-shot remake of *Psycho.* I never cover my mouth mid-moan, but I often wake up screaming in reverse. I start a Daniel Johnston cover band between my hips and cover the pillows with the memory from the afternoon at the lake.

Cover Band

I would totally fuck up Jolene from that song "Jolene."

I Still Like That Movie Where Nicolas Cage
Plays Nicolas Cage

I don't know
which came first: me shaped
like mountains
or mountains born men,
waking next to lost coastlines
     or the words
I love you heard through
     a television set,
or maybe the first
time words woke up,
     the night the streets
turned feral, when outside
was nothing
     but wild children
dressed in masks of wilder children.

The years pass, but the clouds
fit the same.   Every time I think
about trees
it was last night.

I have never been to Toronto,
but I drink champagne
                straight from the bottle.
I repeat the morning
        where you wake me
up by kissing
me on the chin
                        and everything
that follows: the side effects
        of hips
pressed against hips,
and my legs,
the stretch of strangeness,
while off in another language,
a missile points at another missile,
a kidney packed in ice
        is sold at a rummage sale,
and down the block,
        while a mountain naps
at the edge
        of the wilderness,
 a toy gun pretends
to be a real boy.

Poem Written on the Notes App on My iPhone While Sitting on the Couch Watching *Sesame Street* with My Daughter

Today, the forecast calls for a thirty-seven percent chance of thoughts and prayers. In Kennesaw, Georgia, it's illegal for the head of every household to not own a gun. Nine-hundred and fifty miles to the north, it's illegal to live to puberty. My six-month-old daughter sits in her highchair and ghostwrites my poems while I spend the afternoon walking ghosts home from school. How do you background-check a rollercoaster? Can you buy a pony with a .50-caliber mounted on its back? Imagine going to Olive Garden and finding a bullet in your fettuccine Alfredo. Studies show in most states it's easier to become a cop than a barber. Studies show that each study is more depressing than the last. Instead of strapping my daughter into a swing and showing her a map to heaven, I teach her how to dodge bullets by running in the shape of the letter Z. I teach her the difference between a play yard and a graveyard. I ask Siri, *When did the birds stop telling us stories?* Siri doesn't respond. She's taking the rest of the afternoon off. For dinner, I feed my daughter mashed sweet potatoes. Outside, the dog is teaching himself how to howl. Somewhere's somewhere is sending thoughts and prayers, but they keep getting stuck in the clouds. I spend the evening watching my favorite documentary. It's the one where Keanu Reeves sits alone on a bench, feeding stale bread to the pigeons.

Dinosaur Poem Written in June

As we crawl out of lagoons, we realize the dinosaurs are still dead. As we run with the lemmings, the dinosaurs are still dead. And the dinosaurs are still dead as we watch as the sky goes stillborn, as the grass goes stillborn, as everything between the grass and the sky goes stillborn, too. Today, green still looks green. Blue is always a river under sun. Even with the dinosaurs dead, God is still God, though he's feeling pretty worn out. Can you blame him? It's been a long-ass week. It's been a long-ass month. It's been something of a year, a decade, a century of staring at walls, of sleeping in attics, of running from what is hidden under coats. God doesn't like to talk about it. Instead, he sits in his La-Z-Boy, next to a myrrh-scented Yankee Candle that's resting on an end table he got on clearance at Big Lots. God falls asleep in his recliner and dreams of his son's future of nails, of spikes, of thorns. When God wakes up, he is confused. There is so much sharp shit in the world, he doesn't understand how everyone isn't walking around constantly bleeding.

Deleted Scenes from Friday Night Lights

Coach Taylor touches Mrs. Taylor's thigh under the bleachers. Half of Texas carries a purse made out of guns. The other half drinks Lone Stars in the alley behind Buddy's car dealership where Buddy Garrity keeps his side piece's side piece. Jason Street wrestles a shark seventeen kilometers off the coast of Mexico while Julie finds E. coli in an order of cheese sticks at Applebee's. Tim Riggins spends a week pretending to be a virgin. It doesn't go well. Lyla Garrity plants republicans in her Bible. She goes to Emory instead of Vanderbilt, though no one notices. Sometimes when Landry is walking down the street and staring at gravel or grass or track four of *Slanted and Enchanted*, people think he's Matt Damon without the Photoshop or Instagram filters. Two percent of the world's population disappears, but that's a different show. *Clear eyes, a hyphenated regret.* Jason Street wakes up next to a wedding cake. Smash Williams stops talking about himself in the third person. After Julie leaves him for an architect, Matt Saracen drops out of the Art Institute of Chicago and moves to New York City to get an MFA at the New School. Coach Taylor wears his whistle to bed. Mrs. Taylor dresses her accent in another accent.

Basketball Twitter Is a Dumpster Fire

If basketball players want to be rappers and rappers want to be basketball players, then do poets want to be novelists and do novelists want to be birds? They sped up the shot clock a couple years ago, but time ticks slower now. Seattle hasn't felt super since the aughts. I sell the film rights to my youth and now every movie starts with a baby born tightening corsets. I vote Jimmy Butler's cheekbones the new poet laureate. My favorite smell is you tucking a tulip behind my ear as you run your fingers up my thigh. I never wait until halftime for you to come over and give me that finger roll. You never eat sushi off my breasts or from the hum above my thighs, and I don't know how I feel about that. Do you remember Bermuda? We never went. Or maybe the powder stuck to our boots in Vail? That wasn't a thing, either. You don't even own boots.

Chris Paul Calls Jake from State Farm
but He Doesn't Answer

Chris Paul thinks it's lonely being Chris Paul. Sometimes Chris Paul gets so lonely he dresses up as Cliff Paul and goes to Whole Foods to see if anyone will recognize him, but no one ever does. Chris Paul doesn't understand why no one answers their phone when he calls anymore. Not Melo. Not Melo's hoodie. Not even Jake from State Farm. When he tries calling LeBron, it doesn't even ring. It just goes straight to voicemail. Occasionally, Dwyane Wade picks up, but he's always too busy filming that game show with the cube that talks, or he's too busy spending time with his wife. Chris Paul can't remember Dwyane Wade's wife's name, though he knows she's a famous actress, and that he used to have a thing for her when he saw her in *Bring It On*. Or maybe it was *Bad Boys II*. Or maybe it was both. Whenever Chris Paul sees her, he's always surprised how she looks the same, like the last twenty years never happened, which makes Chris Paul think about the harshness of decades and if only his body worked the same as hers. *The gravity of age can be a mean motherfucker* is something he would tell someone if they picked up their phone. Chris Paul walks into his study and stands in front of his trophy case. He doesn't understand why he bought a trophy case. Its emptiness deflates him. He wishes he was back at Wake Forest. He wishes he could do it all over again. He wishes he could grow five inches. Chris Paul hums Skee-Lo, but he won't rap the words. He goes into the bathroom and looks at himself in the mirror. *The gravity of age can be a mean motherfucker.* He whispers the words to himself. Every year it's another piece of him that threatens to let go—another injury, another promise of what's still yet to come. This year it's the soreness in his right arm. Before his right arm it was the sore left knee and the sore left foot and the sore left groin and the sore left knee again. Before the injury to his right arm, Chris Paul thought the left side of him was haunted. Now, he thinks it's all of him that's haunted.

Donner Parties in the Mountains

The oxen and horses go first. There are some leftover legs—sharp edges of bone never boiled into gelatin, barely worth a mention, really—but that's about it. After the oxen and horses, it's the dogs. Everything but the paws. Then, it's pinecones and bark before the daughters cry as they kneel over their father, mouths open, bright with flame.

Foreplay

I.

For foreplay, I buy one of Hillary Clinton's pantsuits off eBay and go as *what if* for Halloween. If you wait long enough, even a cloud will rot. I stand at the edge of the swimming pool at the Holiday Inn Express and watch a manatee chase a speedboat. It is easier to buy a gun than adopt a dog, so I buy a gun and rob a pet store. I steal all the puppies. My favorite emotion is Taylor Swift. For our anniversary, my husband gives me a bouquet of femurs. I put them in a casket we use as an ottoman in the living room. I ask Siri if they sell bulletproof onesies. Siri says, *You can't see it, but I'm shrugging right now.* She tells me to wave a wand and pull a rabbit out of a heart. I do, but the rabbit is dead. I vote we get rid of gym teachers and use their salaries to give every kid a bulletproof backpack. I am scared and it's not even night. I tell my daughter she is the wilderness in the movie where the wilderness rips the beards off lumberjacks. I smoke a pack of menthols under a palm tree in the middle of a mirage. I ask Siri if 5G gives you cancer. Siri says, *Cancer gives you cancer.* This morning, I woke up breathing in reverse. Having a one-night stand with Ryan Gosling's abs is my fourth-favorite fantasy. Can you photoshop love? I can't remember the last time I ate butternut squash. I don't even know if I like butternut squash. Whenever I drive through Oklahoma, all I see is cowboys riding glue sticks. I ask Siri how many people fall in love at gun shows. Siri says, *The same amount of people who were born on a Wednesday.* I steal a lake and get run over by a car. If my husband had a twin brother, I'd totally fuck him. My therapist gives me a silver medal for waking up. I'm so good at kissing in Pig Latin, you don't even know. Vampire Weekend is my seventh-favorite band. When I take too much Adderall, my heart gets a migraine. I love it.

II.

For foreplay, my husband and I play Vaccinate the Republican. My husband plays the republican. I always win. Has Venice sunk yet? I keep forgetting to ask. It seems weird to have never dreamt gills. Sweat waters the oak that continues to grow in someone's yard. I am four days of aches and cramps and milk dripping on hardwood floors. Sometimes I worry my regret here. If you plant a knife, nothing will grow. If shrugs could speak, they would sound like my dog carving a history lesson into the dirt. Do people still diagram sentences? For our anniversary, my husband brings home the CliffsNotes for the *Kama Sutra*. We spend the evening turning the bed into a fire hydrant. After, I check the expiration date on the gallon of milk in the fridge, but the date is covered by a forever stamp. I can't remember the last time I stood in an elevator or dipped a chrysanthemum in a mug of hot water. I ask death when it plans on stopping by. Death says it's not sure. I tell death to give me a bit of notice—I want to be dressed appropriately. I sit on a brown leather couch and ask my therapist when my dreams about trees began. He tells me it could've been years ago, maybe months ago, maybe even last night ago. I ask him if he's ever watched a dead breeze push a tree branch back and forth like a metronome. He shakes his head. I tell him, *Me neither.* He says, *That'll be a thirty-dollar copay.* I tell him I left my wallet in the car.

III.

For foreplay, I dress up as Leigh Chadwick and google *Leigh Chadwick*. I buy a report card off the black market so I have something to put on the refrigerator. I follow my husband to bed and get lost in Egypt. If you plant a tree, you will grow a taller tree. If you plant a mood ring, you will grow a Claire's. How do people living in cities built in snow globes breathe? It seems mean to shake someone into a blizzard. On *Sesame Street*, Elmo says, *That's not a book, that's a milk bottle*, and now I'll never need to get an MFA. If I could capitalism, I still wouldn't. If octopuses had guns, the only people alive would be no one. I'm in a broken-bones-and-cracked-ribs kind of mood, so come find me standing in the middle of I-95, drinking Nyquil straight from the bottle. I donate my Pushcart Prize nomination to Goodwill, but Goodwill doesn't want it. They toss it in the trash, next to trickle-down economics and a refurbished Nintendo GameCube. Tomorrow is a forest of deer and ripped straitjackets. I haven't eaten at a Dairy Queen since the Bush administration. That doesn't say anything about earthquakes, but it should. I have an affair with Google Maps, but it still takes me the wrong way home. Whenever my depression runs away, I always find it at the top of an IKEA parking garage. The only thing scarier than a gun is a dentist. In every movie with a dog in it, that dog is probably dead by now. The best part of hell is being forced to watch the devil stretch Rush Limbaugh into an amusement park.

IV.

For foreplay, my husband pretends to be Stephen King writing a blurb for one of my books I haven't written yet. He tells me I am the best book of the year. He tells me I have a good mouth to be a superhero. He traces *This is why words exist* down my spine. He builds us a bed out of smaller beds as I empty my medicine cabinet and bury it in the back yard, between the swing set and thesaurus tree. It's night. The cicadas are angry or horny or tired. It's impossible to tell. In Colorado, during a birthday party on Mother's Day, seven people are shot and shot and shot and shot and shot and shot and shot, and then they are dead. I am scared of everything the ground holds, so I build a bomb shelter. I teach my daughter how to turn ostrich. There aren't enough words for *hide*. Or maybe one word is too many. I never know anymore.

V.

For foreplay, my husband gets into bed dressed as a county fair. The sheets smell like the Midwest. A cloud of musk hangs above us. Someone dipped the ceiling fan in sulfur. Somewhere, far away or maybe not far away, a tornado promises a town nothing ever again. I have started sleeping naked. My husband's eyes run down my spine. I sway to the sound of his breathing: balloons popping after a boy points a BB gun and pulls the trigger, carnies promising prizes of stuffed giraffes and already-dead goldfish floating in plastic baggies. Music that trails the white horses as they rise and fall, so gently, as if they're walking on the moon. Two teenagers at the top of the Ferris wheel, discovering how to make sound for the first time.

VI.

For foreplay, I drip tears but only out of my left eye. My house looks like the first fifteen minutes of every show on HGTV. Spring starts when people begin touching in the woods, but there is no touching because there is no spring because God forgot to pay the electric bill, so we're deep into April and the snow still hasn't even begun to melt. As hard as I try, I can never dream in French or love in flight. Who made the moon so anxious? In Idaho, a middle schooler shoots other middle schoolers. My husband fucks me on a pile of Pogs. I am always surprised by the lack of scarecrows hiding in cornfields. If you squint hard enough, everything looks like a sequel to *Jurassic Park*. I turn my basement into a lake. I watch tadpoles smile like frogs. The rain is coming or it's already here. Snickerdoodles are my fifth-favorite cookie. I wish I had a reason to title every poem "Phoebe Bridgers."

VII.

For foreplay, I make a grocery list and it's nothing but body wash and eggplant emojis and slightly curved cucumbers. My favorite Taylor Swift track is the one where she wraps herself in cotton and wonders through redwoods. Is there anything blood hasn't touched? My seventeenth-favorite orgasm was the night on the couch, knees burning the carpet, teeth clenched as everything inside me opened and opened. I ask Siri, *How long has my chest been an ashtray?* Siri tells me you should never eat rose petals for breakfast. I divorce my husband, so I have a reason to lean against walls and smoke cigarettes again. A solstice later we remarry under linden. We promise to always fuck in the middle of a thunderstorm. We spend our honeymoon driving Uber drivers home from bars. I ask Siri, *Do ghosts ever get bored?* Siri tells me it would be easier to wrestle Andy Kaufman now than it would have been forty years ago. I rarely think about my daughter's feet until I bring them home from daycare. Some laugh tracks are just laugh tracks, and stains are only real if you can see them. My favorite gun is the one that stops working. My therapist asks me, *On a scale of gin to gin and tonic, how are you feeling?* I tell my therapist, *Sometimes I walk into a room, and the room doesn't complain.* I read somewhere that if you plant a lightning bug, it will die. When did quicksand stop becoming a thing? *Please come over,* I tell the clouds. *I need a reason to cough ghosts.*

VIII.

For foreplay, my husband and I take turns playing Operation on each other. No matter where we touch, our hips keep buzzing. It's late September. The ground crunches. Outside, Jack White turns up his amp as he tunes his guitar. When the sky coughs, I imagine a spear puncturing my ribs. The sky smells like a doctor gave it medicine to try to fix it. The light pole down the block from my house tells me another dog has gone missing, but not who found a bullet in their neck today. An entire city takes a bath and drowns. I pour myself a glass of skim milk. I am given a Pulitzer Prize for sweating through my dreams. Spider eggs hatch in my cerebrum. Moments later, the sky falls.

IX.

For foreplay, I go out to the garden and spend the morning planting chrysanthemums stanzas apart. The garden is full of birds and bees and bees stinging birds. The birds are crying from being stung and the bees are dying from leaving their stingers in the birds' feathered hips. The bees are dying so young that they were never given the chance to learn how to properly flirt. The dog runs around the yard chasing his voice. He howls at his howls. By the afternoon, the sky has turned into a lagoon. All of the clouds but one have drowned. The one cloud left looks like a bank robbing itself. My biggest regret is never touching my husband's thigh while trapped in an elevator, stuck between floors, waiting for the firemen to arrive or the elevator's cords to snap, whichever came first. The warning label on the inside of my wedding band reads *Side effects may include falling in love, catching a rash of similes, choking on orgasms, leaving your Blockbuster card in an ATM, and using the words* comely *and* lust *and* necessary *out of context.* Instead of making dinner, my husband and I swim in a pond as ducks throw pieces of week-old bread into our mouths. By evening, the sky has grown too dark to still be a lagoon. It is now too dark to be anything but nothing. I watch the sky as it sits still, as it waits patiently to become something again.

X.

For foreplay, my husband sits next to me on the couch and writes me a love letter. He mails the love letter to me by carrier pigeon. The carrier pigeon gets lost in transit, and it takes a week for the pigeon to get from one side of the couch to the other. When the pigeon finally finds me, I press it against my chest and untie the note from its leg. My lips stay glued as I read the letter: *I like the way you look when you don't know where to look.* I hold my husband's hand as I write a love letter back to him. *It is the best day when our lips spend the afternoon touching.* I strap the note to the pigeon's left leg and send it back on its way. The pigeon flies into the wall on the opposite end of the room. The pigeon drops to the ground. I ask the pigeon if it's okay, but the pigeon doesn't say anything because the pigeon is dead, and you can't say anything when you're dead. My husband starts to get off the couch to pick up the note and dump the pigeon in the trash, but I keep hold of his hand. *Wait,* I tell him. *It's not time to let go yet.*

3

Bump in the Night

I dream you fall out of bed and break your heart and arms and legs and I think some ribs and your skull chips the laminate floor and the laminate floor chips your skull and mostly everywhere you can walk is covered in the lost and found section of the hospital and now you are dead. In the dream I find you moments after you fall. I dial 911. I touch what skin I can find. I check for a pulse. I check for anything I can pretend is breath. In the dream I find nothing. In the dream you have become nothing. When the paramedics arrive, you're already the color of the sheet they drape over you. The medics place you on a gurney and wheel you out the front door. They slide you into the back of the ambulance, which doesn't bother turning on its siren or feel the need to ignore the red of the stoplights or try to catch a speeding ticket. When I wake up, I'm still thinking about you dying. I think about how most of the breaks didn't matter, how most people don't die from a broken arm or a broken leg or a broken pelvis or even a broken back. They don't die from broken thrusts or from a broken-down car on the side of the interstate. Instead, they die from a broken skull, beaten in from a baseball bat, from being filled with more drugs than blood as they're stuck floating and lost and scared.

Day 219

The dead don't bathe. The dead don't gather in hoards. The dead don't sit under thick oak and read *Jane Eyre* or the book filled with scents of orange falling from a sky that lost itself. Instead, the dead read the book with the bull in it. Or maybe it's not a bull but a bear surrounded by yellow wallpaper. It doesn't matter. The dead don't remember. Sometimes the dead masturbate to strange bodies with blurry faces as they fold into end tables that lean against empty walls, and sometimes the dead eat the poets napping in the woods after a morning of gluing birds to paper. The dead don't remember the last time they ate a Pop-Tart. The dead are dead. The dead think light beer tastes like piss. The dead bang their shins against fire hydrants. The dead tape laughter. The dead moonlight as voice actors. The dead Facebook stalk their exes and immediately regret it. The dead are always lonely but not the most lonely.

Sloths

I blinked. And then, because I couldn't remember if I'd blinked, I blinked again. Whenever I think back to this moment, the moment when I couldn't remember if I blinked, I always imagine a pair of sloth paramedics, moving one foot a minute, entering my childhood home, taking a week to get Billy on a stretcher, a month to get him out of the house and into the back of the ambulance, the red lights flashing as the ambulance heads toward the hospital, a hospital staffed with nothing but sloth doctors and sloth nurses and sloths carrying mops and extra lightbulbs and sloths dressed like candy canes earning their mandatory volunteer hours so they can go to sloth college, and how it would be years later, when there was nothing left of Billy, that the sloth doctor would finally pronounce him dead.

How to Spend Your First Week
Being Furloughed from Work

For the first three days, don't leave the house. Spend them in bed, only getting up to use the bathroom or to grab a granola bar from the pantry or to pour a glass of water you forget to drink until all the ice has melted and the water grows lukewarm and the glass is sweating, like it just ran a marathon, or it's stressed out about paying rent, and so the once cold water you poured into the glass tries to run away, and there it goes, the water cascading over the coaster, dripping onto the nightstand. During those first three days, google *hysterical pregnancies*. Google *hot dads wearing BabyBjörns*. Facebook stalk all your ex-boyfriends: four are married, one is engaged, one fell off a mountain, one is halfway to having a kid, one moved to Hollywood and was in a commercial for Crest Whitestrips, and one doesn't have a Facebook account, which leads you to the assumption that he also fell off a mountain. Google *ultrasound pictures*. Google *does space cause death*? Wonder if anywhere is safe if space isn't even safe and space is above everything, circling you and everyone you know, slowly swallowing everything whole. On day four dream worry. Dream nineteen black holes. Dream bloody chests and quarters fitting through the side of a missing cheek. Dream climbing through the hole in his throat. It is dark inside his throat. You don't like it, so you leave. On day five of your furlough there's a storm, something chopped up and raw and filled with lightning, thunder, tornadoes in your lungs, a tsunami off the coast of the neighbor's pool, hurricanes forming in the wishing well at the mall—the sky a madness you trace like one of those pages covered with dots spread out inches apart, where you take a pencil and draw lines connecting one dot to another, creating miniature constellations. On day six wake up to a gasp. On day seven consider getting in your car and heading north on I-75 where, halfway through a state you'll never see again, you'll toss your cellphone and half of your clothes out the window. Decide to become the dictionary of birth. Teach the world how to start over. Smile every time a server refills your coffee mug. Learn how to spell every country in the world. Start a new life in some small town in Michigan. Buy an old, abandoned lighthouse in this small town in Michigan. Sleep on a single bed you carried up the winding staircase to the top of the lighthouse. Spend the rest of your days walking along cliffs and the rest of your nights in the glow of candlelight, watching a spotlight scan the shoreline.

Jesus Auditions to Play Jesus

In a small town in Ohio, Jesus' agent books him an audition at the community theatre to play Jesus in *Jesus Christ Superstar*. Jesus is nervous. He always has trouble remembering his lines, and his father was always too busy writing his memoirs and getting his hands stuck in clay to ever take him to singing lessons. Still, Jesus is a man of passion. For song. For dance. For stage lights and, whenever possible, glitter. And anyway, Jesus knows time is running out. He's already twenty-nine, and he promised his father that if he didn't make it to Broadway by thirty he'd enroll in the local community college and gain his certificate in carpentry, join a union, earn a pension. But Jesus tries not to think about any of that because right now he is on stage, alone, sweating from the neck as he mumbles his way through "What's the Buzz." The casting director cuts Jesus off halfway through the song. He says something Jesus can't make out, but the crease in the casting director's neck looks like a smile so who knows. Jesus bites his lip. Jesus doesn't know. Jesus bites his lip harder until he tastes blood. He closes his eyes and it's a week later. Jesus still hasn't heard from the casting director. No callback, nothing. His agent stops returning his calls. It's December. He's less than a month away from turning thirty. Jesus enrolls in the spring semester at Columbus State Community College. He signs up for Carpentry 101.

The week leading up to the start of the semester Jesus begins having vivid dreams: chipped paint dipped in lead, a goat being bashed in the head, finding six hundred grand buried in Joel Olsteen's capped teeth painted whale bone, a shooting range built in the hallway of a middle school. Jesus doesn't know what any of this means. His father is too busy melting ice caps and building winter tornadoes in the Midwest to ask. Then it's the first day of class and Jesus is standing in front of an electric saw. He stares at the saw. He thinks, *Anything can be sliced open if you have to slice it open.* He thinks, *The Angel of Death was the original Banksy.* He continues to stare at the saw. He imagines what must come next: climbing out of a cave, the sun bright heat, days lost and mismatched, his wrists covered in sawdust.

Shade

According to the NRA, if you drink a Colt 45 while shooting a .45 Colt you will become ninety percent superhero. When did the world get so scary? I used to fear the simple things: snakes, the devil crawling up my leg, aspartame, UTIs. Now, it's bullets and the cost of health. It's keeping my daughter's heart my daughter's heart. It's feeling to feel. What is a 401K and where is it buried? I can't remember when I stopped dreaming in black and white. For foreplay, my husband and I pretend it's our anniversary. I dress up as a misunderstanding. I handcuff him to the bed and go drink dirty martinis in a hotel bar. When I get home, I crawl into my husband's mouth. I stay there for a week. He doesn't charge me rent. If Scientology were real, I wouldn't have a high enough credit score to go clear. If the earth were flat, would Kyrie Irving still be able to make all of Philly flip with one crossover? I tell my husband, *Let's watch* The Truman Show *and kiss under the covers.* He tells me I look best dressed as shade. I say, *Like that one weekend in late May?* He says, *Like the daffodils in the yard. Like a gun buried beneath snow, lost and forgotten.*

Lesson Plan

I scribble an analogy on my bathroom wall: *Dolly Parton is to Mother Teresa as orgasms are to* _____*(think, never meeting a gun in aisle three at Kroger; think, the lump in the throat of your third lover).* I close my eyes and slide my tongue across the back of my teeth as I repeat my four favorite emotions: *cactus, having sex with men shaped like men, marigold, the one Liz Phair album that doesn't suck.* I hoard any hope for eternity. I keep my regret in the cupboard. I spend the seventeen minutes before dusk cutting my memories in half. The next morning, I set up a booth at the farmer's market off Kingston Boulevard, where I sell them for a pantry full of kites, a flirt of wind, a box of dust.

Hint of Color

I am born an ostrich in a bomb shelter in some small town in Iowa. Minutes after my birth, a tornado knocks on the shelter door. *Hello,* the tornado says, *I am here to kill who is supposed to be killed.* I tell the tornado to please come in, please make itself at home, and please excuse the mess, I am new to this world and still dripping with what I slid out with. The tornado is worried about tracking mud on the floor and staining the paint job on the wall by slinging pieces of cow against it, so the tornado never passes the bomb shelter's foyer. I ask the tornado if it came for me and the tornado says, *Love is a color and there is a hint of that in your neck. Let's see where it goes.* I tell the tornado I understand, though I understand nothing. I put on a pot of tea. By the time the water is boiling, the tornado is out of my foyer and walking across the street. Once across the street, the tornado takes two men shaped like bears. Their teeth were full of rot and had to be pulled years earlier. The men kept their dentures soaking in jars on the nightstands next to their beds. They were both named Joe.

Hospital Poem

I wake up as myself and then wake up as another me and then another me says hello to the first or second or eighty-fifth or three-millionth me. A storm brews in the lunchroom, chipping the coffee pot, knocking over a chair. I am wearing a gown covered in charcoal. The walls are padded in foam. I bump into the foam and bounce back and forth like a game of *Pong*. An orderly sprinkles me with salt and leads me toward a set of double doors. We pass a closet filled with jackets shaped like pretzels and white as clouds. An *Applause* sign hanging from the ceiling begins to flash. *Most laugh tracks are a symphony of hyenas or echoes from the dead*, the orderly says. I don't know how I got here. The double doors open. The walls sigh. I don't know how I got here. I close my eyes. A meteor falls from the sky.

Somewhere in the Middle
We Will Fuck Up

You promise to always walk me home

from school   I promise to love you through

the early bird special.

I Think Tumbleweed

The phone rings. When I answer, a hurricane blows through the receiver. I am standing in the kitchen as the wind flings plates against the wall. An ocean forms in the sink, crashing waves against the granite countertop. A chair slides across the living room floor, and I think, *tumbleweed.* I am still thinking *tumbleweed* when the chair smashes through the sliding glass door. The roof begins to rain. An anchor on The Weather Channel walks into my kitchen. *You don't live here,* I tell him. *Get the fuck out.* I keep the phone pressed against my ear and ask the hurricane, *Where did the calmness of my heart go?* I eat my throat as I wait for an answer, as I wait for the wind to slow and the rain to stop. I wait for the eye. I wait for anything. I want for everything. I wait and wait, and I am still waiting until the hurricane turns into a tropical storm and then the tropical storm turns into my medicated depression and I am the only one in this world or the world next to this world with a phone pressed against their ear.

How to Make Water

Regret never being shot out of a cannon. Miss Anthony Bourdain. Miss beginnings and middles and futures. Miss drinking beer in the shower, discovering new words like explorers devouring continents. Miss never needing therapy. Miss dreams that begin with a big bang and single-celled organisms swiping right on Tinder. Miss those same dreams that end with legs stretching down the block. How many days has it been since you lost the instruction manual on how to swallow? Lately, you've been thinking in islands of plastic and fish going *oh shit oh shit oh shit.* A documentary on Netflix tells you that during the inquisition, they referred to opium as *the stuff of the devil.* Regret that night in the garage. Miss possibilities. Miss never. Miss that one pill that still hasn't been invented yet. Miss soon. Miss saying, *Soon I will never be sick.*

How to Be a Poet Days After Finding Out
Your Husband Cheated on You

On the patio, smoke another Turkish Silver. Toss the butt into the back yard. Imagine a forest fire as the cherry fizzles, as the grass stays grass. Go inside and throw what's left of the pack of Turkish Silvers in the trash. Microwave a frozen burrito. Fish out the pack of cigarettes from the trash. Take two Xanax. Forget about the burrito in the microwave. Stare at the bottle of Xanax. Take another then take a shower. Turn the water so hot your body turns Dante. Don't bother drying off. Still wet, get in bed anyway. Think this is the last time you might ever be wet. Try to masturbate. Get close three times but don't finish. Give up. Turn on the TV. Watch part of an infomercial for a knife that can cut through a penny. Change the channel. Catch the last half of a commercial for a movie called *Space Death*, where a knife cuts through a star and then the screen goes black and then the tagline: *This Thanksgiving Not Even Space Is Safe*. Think you would rather have a knife that could cut through a star than a penny. Think about not thinking. It's five in the afternoon. Fall asleep. Dream the two of them in his Volvo, parked in her driveway, his forehead pressed against the steering wheel, his throat slit from a knife that can cut through a star or a penny or maybe both.

How to Make It to One Day, Five Years Later

For Halloween, dress up as a wet dream. Buy an Easy-Bake Oven off the dark web. Go into the back yard and plant a banana. Wait for the banana to push through the earth, sprouting bark and leaves and other bananas. Six months later there is a banana tree. Pull a banana off the banana tree. Dip the banana in a bowl of chocolate. Smell sound as it loses its taste. Remember when things used to be worth calling *things*, when every emotion rhymed with *thigh* and everything touched ended stained in sweat: the couch, the bathroom counter, the kitchen counter, the back seat of the car, the grass circling the lake. Now, every breakfast tastes like a Jack Johnson song. Now, the baby is crying. Imagine going into the other room so you could be the person who goes into the other room. But you can't go into the other room because the baby is still crying. Instead, drop a glass of orange juice. Pretend it's an accident. Look at the baby with wide eyes and say, *Oops*. Say, *Oh my*. Stare at the shards of glass, pulp, a lake shaded summer. Don't wipe up the spilt juice. Instead, watch the lake turn rivulets as it flows through the cracks in the tile floor, looking for an escape.

You

You, weather balloon. You, the Holiday Inn Express off Kingston Pike. You, highways and continental breakfasts and two-ply. Mismatched socks. An em dash stuck in the fire lane of a Trader Joe's parking lot. The Sunday edition of *The New York Times* crossword puzzle. You, the most southern part of my collarbone. All thrust and salary. Vortex. Husband. Unlocked doors. A diagram of three ways to fall off a cliff. You, gun control. You, cake. You, Oxford comma. You, Keto. You, hit and run. You, chest hair. A sweaty interlude. Mellifluous. Much. The tenth anniversary of the night at the bar. A county fair trapped in the snow globe hidden in a larger snow globe. A Sunday matinee. A crushed pack of menthols.Track three through eight of *The Moon & Antarctica*. The basement of a robin's nest. You, hand soap. You, bar soap. You, lavender body wash. You, meaning. You, *nom de plume*. Every synonym of *touch*. Comma. Fire alarm. Comma. Senate majority. Period. You, a coupon for a package of Crest Whitestrips. You, the second heart of an octopus. A chilled salad fork. You, hit record. You, millennium. You, cellar door.

The Poem of Tiny Clouds

Legs and everything above them. Spread angel in an open field. Voice pointing toward the sky. Blades of grass tickling the back of her neck. Blades of grass making her legs itch as she blows on a dandelion, watching tiny clouds form just inches from her lips. Sweat down her chest. August thighs. Then, the moon and the stars and her finger stretching toward heaven as she counts the dots freckled gleam. She loses count before she can make it to infinity. She knows some words are too big to mean anything. Still, she stretches her finger further into the sky, convinced she won't lose count this time.

How to Bruise a City

On Sunday evenings, dress up like Scripture. In bed, on your back, stare at the cracks on the ceiling. Imagine an upside-down earthquake, someone sawing the sky apart. Your husband climbs on top of you, runs a heater across your abdomen. When he goes down on you, grip the night in his hair. He bites your left thigh but not your right. Wrap your legs around the back of his neck, turn pretzel as his tongue stretches mountains continents apart, parts oceans, turns water into more water. After, fall asleep on a raft in the middle of the Seine. Dream sheep eating wolves while the moon files for divorce from poetry. Wake up an architect. Build a rollercoaster down your husband's spine with your tongue. Construct skyscrapers south of his collarbone, bridges over his rib cage. After building a new city, go into the kitchen. The kitchen smells like French toast but you only have pancake mix. Eat a spinach omelet you don't remember making. Drink a mimosa out of a coffee mug. Take a shower. In the shower, press your thumb against the bruise on your left thigh, now blackened and purple. Close your eyes. Taste your lips as you grip your right thigh, wishing for the same.

Volcano Poem

I should watch less movies. I should love more. I should learn how to slow the fuck down. I have learned there is only so much magic in medicine, only so much a mask can cover, that most of my poems mention hieroglyphics and I don't know why, and that volcanoes can cause thunderstorms now, it's a thing, or maybe it was always a thing, so says the article you read to me on your iPhone while we let our pillows do the jobs they were hired to do. It's late into the night and the night yawns. Every leap year I dream snakes curled into fireplaces. The next morning, I wake up three pages and end with a bullet in the brain. If you live long enough, everything is a gun or something that looks like a gun. I mentioned volcanoes, but did I mention the lack of green in Greenland? Or the mass grave buried under the library in a Colorado suburb? America is still just as shitty as it was yesterday, as it was the day before yesterday, as it was a hundred years ago yesterday, yet the birds are still here, yet Jennifer Lopez and Ben Affleck are still in love, and yet, even so, the old man dressed like Santa is still standing in front of Macy's, ringing a copper bell, smiling at his empty red bucket.

Daughters of the State

[Redacted] hasn't had the scent of baby formula on her wrist in months. With each additional syllable she digs herself a new grave. At night [Redacted] dreams of ants and how they can carry ten times their own weight. Or is it a hundred times their own weight? A thousand? [Redacted] can't remember. It doesn't matter. Her dreams don't care. All her dreams know is that there are ants and every Thursday they carry the entire afternoon on their backs. When [Redacted] wakes up, her first thought is that she would kill the sun if she could reach it. [Redacted] imagines wading into an empty ocean, building a paper airplane and flying through a sky as stale as cardboard. [Redacted] thinks about what she wanted to tell her father before he pointed the gun at her mother: *Bullets need vacations too.*

Department of Children Services

The weather a memory too busy getting drunk and lost, getting high and lost, getting fucked and lost, to ever remember the giving of birth and the having of children, their blood thicker than tree sap, fire surrounding their cages of ribs, the dead leaves under their feet as they wander through a forest, any forest, the craving of the rustle of bush of one body under another, and when I see them, they tear out their eyes and for a moment, they are no longer lost—they are no longer.

A Library of Limbs

The Second Amendment says I am the Second Amendment. The pastor says thoughts and prayers. The wind says I am tired of carrying the smell of death. Some senators say too soon, too soon. Some senators say now is never the time. Some senators say now is the only time. The Second Amendment says everyone should buy a gun out of the trunk of a car in a Starbucks parking lot. The gun show says we're having a BOGO sale on body bags. The wind says I am also tired of carrying the sound of death. Mississippi says put a gun in your waistband when you go to Kroger to buy a gallon of skim and a package of Pampers. Tennessee says let's be more like Mississippi. California says puff, puff, pass. Texas says at least we're not Florida. Colorado says well, fuck. Colorado says did you not see the library of limbs. Colorado says sorry about the spilt blood in the produce aisle. Colorado says the popcorn is on us. The ghosts say there is no more room in the haunting place. The wind says still, it's the smell that's the worst. The South says if only. The Second Amendment says I will always be the Second Amendment. All senators say thoughts and prayers. Thoughts and prayers say sorry we are so useless. Jesus says if I had a gun that fucking cross wouldn't have stood a chance.

Brief Excerpts from *Leigh Chadwick Is Your Favorite Poet: An Unauthorized Biography*, Written and Edited by Leigh Chadwick

I.

Leigh Chadwick reaches into her chest and finds her heart swollen. She reaches below her abdomen and finds the loneliest parts of her a peach. Leigh Chadwick has stopped counting in weeks, minutes, voices sent through the mail. She keeps an *Out of Order* sign over her heart whenever she walks through the produce aisle at Publix. Leigh Chadwick makes herself a cardigan even the moths ignore. She never has to pay for drugs when she flirts with the busser at Olive Garden. Leigh Chadwick knows that if you drive one way for too long you will eventually drown.

II.

It is a lonely June night, probably 2014, though maybe it's 2013, when Leigh Chadwick leaves the bar, gums bleached in rum, walking down Kingston Boulevard, sobering the lust of leftover tongue drying on the nape of her neck, and then she is home, alone, where she is met with nothing but the daddy longlegs creeping across the ceiling and the floor below it, swaying back and forth from the tide of an ocean miles away, and finally, the sound of a hair dryer flirting with the bathtub.

III.

Leigh Chadwick sits on a bench that looks like a bench outside the funeral home that looks like a Baptist church. Leigh Chadwick can't move or she doesn't want to move or maybe both are the same thing. Either way, Leigh Chadwick can't get herself off the bench that looks like a bench. *Just go*, she tells herself. *Just get the fuck up and go.* But Leigh Chadwick doesn't go. Instead, Leigh Chadwick sits and sits and sits, and as Leigh Chadwick sits and sits and sits, she thinks, *I am very good at sitting*, and then someone is running a hand through her hair and then the someone who is running a hand through her hair is saying, *Just stay here.* The someone is saying, *I'll go*, and then the someone is inside the funeral home that looks like a Baptist church that also moonlights as season three of *The Walking Dead*, and then the someone is picking out a coffin while Leigh Chadwick is still outside, sitting on the bench that looks like a bench. She stares at her shoes. They are average shoes—brown, suede, scuffed. She imagines the average shoes saying, *I have walked over so much. I have touched what you are feeling.* Leigh Chadwick imagines the shoes, so average in length and width, saying, *Someone is always dead or dying or thinking about dying.* Leigh Chadwick reaches into her purse and takes out a green BIC, a yellow pack of American Spirits, and though she has no one to say it to, she still says, *Everything has a color*, as she puts a cigarette between her lips and tries to flick the lighter with her thumb, but her hands are shaking and no matter how hard she tries, no matter how many times her thumb runs along the ridges of the lighter, she can't get the cigarette lit.

IV.

Today Leigh Chadwick's horoscope is the memory of the night at the bar, the humidity from an open window in the women's bathroom and her back pressed against the wall as a boy crawls through her, planting tulips in her spine, whispering every word that rhymes with *mellifluous* in her ear as his fingertips—calloused, swollen—trace the rhythm of the sea down her chest, and then she's outside, standing in the middle of the gin-soaked parking lot, her head between her knees and her lungs scraping the enamel off her teeth as the crisp sheet of night covers whatever the boy next to her is about to say.

V.

Leigh Chadwick stands under a tent, next to a priest who's next to a mahogany box. The mahogany box goes lower than the ground. The service is shorter than an episode of a sitcom. On the way home, the limousine stops at a red light. Leigh Chadwick thinks about what there is to say when there is nothing left to say. Someone's hand reaches for hers. *There is no one to make a casserole for*, the someone says. They both close their eyes.

VI.

After college, Leigh Chadwick puts her emotions in a safe, throws away the key, rents a fishing boat, and drops the safe in the middle of the Atlantic. She watches the water around the safe seltzer as it goes Jules Verne. For years, the safe stays oceans deep, until the night at the bar when you order her the entire bar and then invite her back to your apartment and when she gets there, to your one-bedroom cardboard box, she knows before you know she knows that she is never going to leave. Months later, when you ask if she wants to start keeping some of her clothes in one of your dresser drawers, Leigh Chadwick says yes because she is in love and love makes you say things like yes, even to empty dresser drawers, or maybe especially to empty dresser drawers. So Leigh Chadwick takes scuba lessons, gains her certification, rents a wet suit and an oxygen tank and takes the same fishing boat back out to the middle of the Atlantic, in search of the safe she left for the ocean to swallow years before. After weeks of expeditions, fistfights with sharks, and pulling heart after heart after heart out of octopuses, Leigh Chadwick finds the safe. It is painted coral and covered in crabs and what grows on the sides of abandoned boats. Leigh Chadwick hauls the safe back to her apartment and borrows a power drill from a neighbor with a neckbeard who wears deodorant that smells like maple syrup. It takes days of drilling before she finally cracks the safe. Somehow, the inside is still dry. Leigh Chadwick takes her emotions out of the safe and carries them into the kitchen. She sets them on the counter and takes the cheese grater out of a cabinet. She shaves her emotions down into thin ribbons that she uses to garnish over a bowl of Kraft Macaroni & Cheese. Leigh Chadwick eats her emotions with a spoon. After, she packs a small suitcase with clothes and drives to your apartment, where she unpacks the small suitcase of clothes in the bottom drawer of your dresser. It starts with one dresser drawer and then turns into a dresser drawer and half of a closet, and then you ask her to move in with you and because love makes you say things like yes, Leigh Chadwick says yes, and then after the pregnancy test that shows two lines—followed by three more tests, which also show two lines, because *just in case*, because *that shit can be faulty, you know?*—you take her to Planned Parenthood and the doctor says, *Congratulations, you're very pregnant! You could not possibly be more pregnant*, and Leigh Chadwick grips your hand and starts to cry, and it is a good cry, though it is ugly and full of snot.

VII.

Leigh Chadwick moves to a state so red you can't tell if you're bleeding. A state where everyone spends their days staring at the sky as people fly over them. Leigh Chadwick takes a nap and wakes up married, a thirty-year mortgage tied around her wrist. A baby glued to her chest. A pair of lips blowing smoke rings. She finds your hands a wonder. She hides your medicine in the lockbox of her lungs. A song too famous not to hum plays in the background as Leigh Chadwick spends her Saturday afternoons washing the dirt off a garden in the kitchen sink.

VIII.

Every time Leigh Chadwick closes her eyes, she sees a dead animal on the side of the road. A deer. A dove. A duck. A dodo. A Danger Mouse B-side. It doesn't matter what animal; the animal is always dead—nothing but patches of skin and fur covering what skin and fur was always meant to cover. *Some.* A word. *One.* Another word. *Everything is always a word, and a word is always one* is a thought Leigh Chadwick has. When Leigh Chadwick closes her eyes, the dead animal is tattooed on the back of her eyelids. A duck-billed platypus. A dog hiding from a missing poster taped to every light pole down the block and the block next to that block. Somewhere, someone is crying. Somewhere, something howls. *I breathe in the most obvious tenor* is another thought Leigh Chadwick has. Leigh Chadwick likes to walk when she's not driving, but today she's driving. The sign off Highway 61 reads *Fallen Rocks.* There is no *Beware!* in front of *Fallen Rocks.* There is no *Warning!* There is just one word plus one word: *Fallen* and then *Rocks.* Leigh Chadwick keeps her hands on the wheel, ten and two. She looks for rocks, the fallen kind, but only sees patches of grass, a Shell station that died a decade before, back when the world was shitty but maybe a little less shitty. Leigh Chadwick blinks and there's a turtle on the side of the road, upside down, turned inside out. Leigh Chadwick tries to remember the days before she learned what it meant to blink. She can't remember. The days, she feels, were so long ago. Leigh Chadwick realizes she can't remember much: The morning she watched the body bags pile on top of each other, like clumps of coal. Or the morning Oklahoma fell off the map. Or which song was playing through the loudspeakers when Waco turned into an afternoon barbecue. Instead of discovering facts, Leigh Chadwick turns off Highway 61 and spends the afternoon in a Macy's fitting room, trying on metaphors and similes. Leigh Chadwick is a check engine light. Leigh Chadwick is a piece of gum you swallowed three years ago. Leigh Chadwick stands in front of the dressing room mirror. She keeps herself straight, stiff. The hair on her skin turns needles. She holds her breath. She knows if she does this long enough, her blood will turn sweet and thick—a brown malaise— and that she will turn into a tree. But Leigh Chadwick breathes deeply. She bends and stretches. She tries on a chimney from the 1940s. She tries on a black dress that looks like a third date. Leigh Chadwick is a universal remote. She is an *out of the office* email. Leigh Chadwick closes her eyes. When she opens them, she is standing at the checkout counter. She buys a dress shaped like a dress. As she leaves the mall, Leigh Chadwick promises to learn how to pray again. She doesn't know what that means. Leigh Chadwick has never seen an olive that wasn't drunk. She doesn't know what that means, either. Leigh Chadwick feels nothing whenever she hears the word *smog*, though she once ate an entire package of grapes without rinsing them off. Another time she let a candle burn in the foyer while she went out to check the mail. She knows what that means but decides it doesn't matter. Nothing matters until it does. And then Leigh Chadwick is back in her car, heading out of the parking lot, her hands ten and two on the wheel as she merges back onto Highway 61. Her eyes sting. She wants to rub them. She wants to blink. Instead of blinking, Leigh Chadwick thinks about the Macy's fitting room—the stiffness of her back, the shortness of her breath, the sap that began to leak out of her skin as her body turned linden.

IX.

Leigh Chadwick puts sunscreen on the sunflowers in the yard. She builds her poems into tree houses. A butterfly cocoons. Inside the house, Leigh Chadwick dresses up as a lifeguard while you go scuba diving in the washing machine. She plugs in an iron and coats your clothes in butter. The television in the family room is tuned to CNN. Someone is shot somewhere. In the chest. In the throat. In the throat of their chest. Somewhere else, someone is shot. In the leg. In the back of the head. In the middle of a storm named after someone's brother. Leigh Chadwick grows a migraine. Everything is the news even when it's not. It's late afternoon. A Sunday. Leigh Chadwick wants to ask you if you think ghosts go on dates, neck in the back seat of cars, fuck against splintered oak. Instead, she says, *What a nice day for a drive, don't you think?* and you nod and then the two of you are on Highway 61, passing the pawn shop across from the leftover rubble of the last Toys "R" Us, and then the billboard that reads *DID YOU GROW UP WITH NICE PEOPLE?* Leigh Chadwick thinks about the billboard, the question on the billboard, and she doesn't know. She's never been good at answering questions that aren't multiple choice. Leigh Chadwick licks her lips, runs her tongue along her gums. Her mouth tastes like a palindrome. She stares outside the passenger's side window. It's nothing but trees and trees and more trees—all of them so full and green and wide awake. Leigh Chadwick thinks if the sky wasn't close to setting, it could be morning. She imagines counting the trees, counting to a thousand and then going until she reaches a thousand thousands. She can taste the word *foliage.* She can smell the butter on your thighs. Leigh Chadwick thinks, *Lush, a shade of deep love.*

X.

And on the seventh day God says, *Here, take it. Take it all. It is yours,* and Leigh Chadwick tells God, *Thanks, God, but I'm good. I've got a snickerdoodle to eat and a husband to go crawl inside,* and then Leigh Chadwick finishes eating her snickerdoodle and wipes the crumbs off her hands with a paper towel and then crawls down your throat, where she swaddles the robin's nest in your chest as you put on a pair of cotton pajamas and brush your teeth with lavender.

XI.

This is spring and it glows. Everything is covered in linden. Even the linden is covered in linden. Leigh Chadwick is here, right here, also covered in linden, stuck between these walls, in a house built a grandma ago, where it is so easy for her to be with you. *I love you*, the chest inside her says. *I love you*, your voice outside the walls echoes back. Leigh Chadwick's eyes wild children, your chest holier than church. There are moments and there are moments. Leigh Chadwick doesn't know which moment this is. She doesn't know if it matters. She assumes it doesn't. Outside, spring continues glowing linden. Leigh Chadwick steeps tea in her underwear while she imagines you sliding your hands over her hips, down her thighs. She brushes her teeth for two full minutes. She swishes Listerine between her cheeks. Leigh Chadwick goes through her closets and picks out a sundress that bloomed last week. The threads have already begun to wilt. Her throat presses against her gums. Leigh Chadwick considers praying again, though she never prayed a first time.

XII.

Monogamy is buying a gun and watching your lover swallow all the bullets. This is what Leigh Chadwick thinks as she lies in bed, listening to the thunder outside her window. It's night, late enough to almost be called morning. A streak of light cracks through the blinds. Whenever Leigh Chadwick sees lightning, she imagines God taking a picture. The sky has been threatening to open for hours, and it finally does. Leigh Chadwick's hands keep fiddling with themselves like they're brand-new lovers. Oh, how they flirt. Oh, how they are filled with impossible passion with nowhere to go. Leigh Chadwick thinks, *Or maybe monogamy is having someone to tell you where your hands should go.* Everything outside has turned into wind. Leigh Chadwick listens to the trees hum as she stares at the ceiling, waiting for the kernels to pop.

XIII.

Leigh Chadwick goes into the bathroom, turns off all the lights and spins around three times while chanting, *Leigh Chadwick, Leigh Chadwick, Leigh Chadwick.* When she turns the lights back on, a poem has appeared on the bathroom mirror. It is a good poem. Leigh Chadwick types the poem into the Notes app on her iPhone. She titles the poem "Craft Essay" and submits it to the *Paris Review.* She sits on the toilet and doom-scrolls through Twitter as she waits three hundred and seventy-six days for a form rejection from a literary journal based in a city she can't afford to live in and named after a city she will never be able to afford to visit.

Epilogue

The Questionnaire of Good Intentions

1) Where are you?

A. Trapped in a castle, waiting for someone with a plunger to come beat the giant turtle with spikes sticking out of his shell. Please send help!
B. In a spaceship, heading toward the sun. It is hard to breathe in the spaceship. I can feel my skin melting. Please send help!
C. I don't know, but I feel pretty okay here.
D. Who cares? There's a fridge full of Stella.

2) What did your first love smell like?

A. A free sample of Calvin Klein Obsession from the fragrance section at Macy's.
B. ~~The flowers in his beard that he grew and grew and grew so he could take pictures of himself lying in an empty field with the sole purpose of posting said photos on his Insta-gram page.~~ Austin, TX.
C. Day two of the Fyre Festival.
D. N/A

3) What did your second love smell like?

A. A package of dryer sheets.
B. LOL
C. ~~The same as the first love.~~ Madison, WI.
D. N/A

4) What did falling in love feel like?

A. An emptied recycling bin.
B. The third, maybe fourth Bright Eyes album.
C. Standing in the eye of a hurricane, waiting patiently.
D. N/A

5) What did falling out of love feel like?

A. Moving to Florida and not being allowed to leave.
B. The third, maybe fourth Bright Eyes album.
C. Watching Warner Herzog listen to the audio recording of a bear eating that guy in the documentary about a bear eating that guy.
D. N/A

That One Week in Cedar Rapids, Iowa

My feet are cold. They remind me of that one week in Iowa. I look at my feet. I don't like to think about that week in Iowa. It was not a good week in Iowa. I keep looking at my feet. They are covered in cotton—frayed and tubed. I can feel every inch of me forgetting something important. This happens often, whether my feet are cold or if I'm drinking a beer in the shower or if I'm watching you watching yourself in the mirror as you straighten the knot in your tie. I put on a second pair of socks. Our daughter was sleeping and now she's not. Our daughter is tired of being tired. Yesterday, she was small and today she is still small but less small than yesterday's small. I imagine her as yeast in an oven. I imagine our daughter continuing to expand, the growth that will come, the growth that has come, the growth that is coming right now. I don't remember the stork because there never was a stork. Just the *breathe*. Just the *push*. Just the stitches. I look at the mobile above the crib. The tiger is catching up to the elephant. I wonder if our daughter will ever learn the word *ivory*.

Based on a True Story

Once upon a time, love was a polka dot dress and a drawing of a cave on the inside of a cave. The polka dot dress and the cave drawing touched everywhere. They touched under street lamps. They touched in empty parking lots, and they touched in crowded parking lots. They touched on roller coasters and in the middle of driving ranges, the golf balls bouncing off them like mosquitos. They touched while standing in line at Starbucks, and they touched while standing in line at Target. They touched on top of the sheets they bought after standing in line at Target, and they touched under the sheets they bought after standing in line at Target. They touched while they were touching. It was a sweaty touch. A pizza-for-breakfast touch. A rain-from-the-leaking-roof touch. They touched until they were so thirsty they drank the rain from the leaking roof of touch. They touched after they drank the rain from the leaking roof. They touched until they made themselves thirsty again.

Chocolate Chip Pancakes

I want to be polite in the way people who sneeze into their elbows are polite, so I always look both ways before driving into the ocean. I feel useless holding an empty wine glass, so I'm always buying more bottles of wine, which means I'm always stumbling into walls and falling into my bathtub as I reach for my hair dryer to steady myself. I often wake up expecting to see rocks shaped like atomic bombs, or atomic bombs shaped like rocks, or the devil crawling out of a sewer grate—his pitchfork a forest fire the color of California. Sometimes life is just a whimper. Sometimes life is nothing. Sometimes, after I finish my chocolate chip pancakes, the devil gives me lightning bolts shaped like toothpicks. I want to be polite in the way automatic doors rarely stop being automatic, so I tell the devil, *Thank you*, as I take a lightning bolt and close my eyes, waiting for the world to melt.

Utah Is a Documentary

Out west, saints climb ladders. Depending on who you ask, the ladders are either tall or heaven is low. Sometimes it's always morning. You ask me to follow you home. *I love you.* Your words. The snow hasn't melted yet, and I haven't been outside since I was told I could go outside. *Everything is safe*, the talking heads say, but I don't know. I don't know if I want to know. There are so many questions I want to ask: *Am I still allowed to laugh? Are people still upset about straws? Are you still allowed to laugh?* What I really want to know is why there aren't enough lips to kiss what we've lost. You don't answer your phone anymore. I've stopped caring about the way people smell. My mental health tells me stories around the campfire in the middle of my bedroom. Thunder sutures itself through my spine. The sky coughs flakes of dandruff. I dream I pull your teeth, rest my head on your decaying chest. I wake up a decade of lust. I wake up blank. I wake up dressed in a robe that makes my skin smell like wildflowers. It's Tuesday. You would never be here. I go into the kitchen and put on a pot of tea.

The Study of Sky

I peel the epidermis off the blade of a sword. I drain the Seine. I have a baby so I can learn how to hold a baby. I disinfect light switches and toss out the milk that spoiled last Tuesday. I cut the alphabet in half, light bottle rockets in the basements of my exes. I learn the patience of a Thursday afternoon. When I look up, I watch a loon touch the precipice of where a tree no longer stays a tree. Of where it becomes sky. Of where the words *before* and *after* meet. I ask you to please excuse the chipped paint on the front door, the alarm clock flashing eights, the dust on the mantle. I pluck your hair from the sides of my ribs. I thank you for coming to my TED Talk. I thank you for visiting my grave as I grow antlers that curve like calligraphy. I wade into my own wilderness—thick brush of the dead and dying, an underbelly of song.

One Times Nine

Also known as the RIP bullet, the Radically Invasive Projectile is considered by many to be the deadliest bullet manufactured for public use. Each Radically Invasive Projectile contains nine separate "wound channels." I don't know what that means. Google tells me it means you can never have enough bullet in your bullets. Google tells me it means that when an RIP hits you, expect your organs to explode on contact. Google tells me this is because every kid has the same amount of organs. Because no one is born with a bulletproof brain or bulletproof lungs or a bulletproof funny bone or a bulletproof liver or bulletproof kidneys or a bulletproof heart. Because who needs a spleen. Hell, I don't even know what a spleen does. Google tells me your spleen spell checks your blood, which seems important enough, though Google also says, like with spell check, a spleen is something you can live without. I stand in the middle of an empty classroom and imagine my daughter folded origami under a desk while Google informs me that a Radically Invasive Projectile promises efficiency. Because one bullet should do the work of nine. Because reloading is only fun when there's nowhere left for them to run. Because on to the next. Because the unemployment rate is high. Because the unemployment rate is low. Because efficiency cuts costs. Because people do people things. Because if you cut a casket in half, you can bury two kids for the price of one.

Pudding Poem

During morning announcements, the principal comes on the PA and tells the student body, *If you survive the semester, you will automatically receive straight A's.* Today feels like a meteor or public execution. I want to get knocked on the head and fall into a coma so I don't have to see how the day ends. I want to wake up in a hospital on a Thursday that bleeds into a Sunday. I want to eat chocolate pudding by the gallon. For foreplay, my husband pours Southern Pecan down the bullet hole in my neck. He licks the foam that comes back up and runs down my chest. Outside, everything is blue or black or a dark cape that is neither blue nor black. On CNN, the chyron reads, *Blink twice if you see the bomb coming.* Then: *Blink thrice if your nose itches.* That night, I dream my childhood bathroom is infested with ladybugs. I dream the boy with the neck and arms and face and elbows and stomach he filled with bleach is dead. I dream a group of miniature ghosts in an empty field. The ghosts say they are all sad they weren't able to graduate from playground and move on to puberty and first touches. They sit in a circle and play duck, duck, goose. The ghosts tell me no one wants to be the goose. They tell me that with the right heart, you can kill anything twice.

Molt

I have never held a hand that didn't sweat, but every morning I wake a body full of aches. I do not know how to define *dance* or the age of the earth. I don't even try. Instead, I divide myself into months subtracted by days. Minutes go pi. I water my mattress and watch the tulips bloom. *I love the word magnolia*, I say, the ending of a ghost story I tell to an empty room. The earth burns as it cries as it willows into a soaked pillowcase. I kneel where I once stood. There is no longer a stream. There are no white horses or carnies peddling dead goldfish wrapped in plastic baggies. There is no baby, swathed in cotton. I don't know how to finish sentences I don't mean. *The good news is dot dot dot.* I am alone, alone as the meaning always meant, quieting the already silent—as quiet as both of my parents, as quiet as both of my grandparents, as quiet as both of my grandparents' parents—so I memorize every synonym of *hush*: my lover's arrows scattered across an empty parking lot, my mouth as I hide from what falls under the awning of a bus stop, every emotion grown skylark, even the song the songbird dreams into a fallen cloud.

Every Year Is a Year

It's 2015, the Monday after that third weekend in May, when you walk into my heart and forget to come out. I don't complain. I am happy for you to stay, to build a house in my chest, to plant sunflowers in my lungs, and it is in this field of sunflowers where you ask me, *If a train leaves Seattle at 3 p.m. and is going 60 miles per hour, and, at exactly the same time, a famine in Paris, Texas, clogs a hummingbird's lungs and the hummingbird coughs and coughs and the hummingbird is out of breath and so the hummingbird flies to the ER, where the receptionist tells the hummingbird it's going to be a seven-hour wait, at what moment does a Thursday bleed into a Friday?* and I tell you, *I failed calculus but my lawyer is an expert in maritime law, so I only rob banks in the Bermuda Triangle.* This makes enough sense for June to smell like a National Book Award. And then it's August, and I am sticking a forever stamp onto the top left corner of a postcard with scarecrows playing hide and seek throughout the Midwest on the front. I mail the postcard to *That Place Where Adrienne Lives*, but the postcard gets lost and ends up in a P.O. Box in a ghost town trapped in a snow globe. For Labor Day, everyone pretends the ice caps aren't melting into bottles of Evian. Then, it's Halloween, and I am teaching you how to lobotomize a stanza. You mess up twice, but no one notices. I spend November packing boxes into larger boxes.

On the fifth of December, we move seven states north, into an apartment with an extra bedroom neither of us ever go into. For Christmas, in place of stockings, you hang empty medicine cabinets over the mantle. New Year's is the stretch in your moan. I spend the first month of 2016 watching the earth slowly empty itself. You ask if it's a leap year. I tell you I don't know. You don't care enough to find out. I drink a glass of water. You dress up like a universal remote and climb into bed. I press the *rewind* button on your left hip and then it's 2015, the Monday after the third weekend in May, and you are walking.

Acknowledgments

Thank you to the editors of the following journals in which some of these poems, often in different form, originally appeared: $—Poetry is Currency; Bear Creek Gazette; Cease, Cows; The Daily Drunk; Emerge Literary Journal; CLOVES Literary; Gone Lawn; HAD; Heavy Feather Review; Hobart; Identity Theory; The Indianapolis Review; The Jarnal; Malarkey Books; No Contact; Olney Magazine; One Art; Pithead Chapel; Pontoon; Rejection Letters; Reservoir Road Literary Review; Revolution John; Salamander; Schuylkill Valley Journal; scissors & spackle; Scrawl Place; Sledgehammer Lit; Stanchion Lit; Twin Pies Literary; W&S Quarterly; Whale Road Review; and Unbroken.

"Daughters of the State" first appeared in the chapbook *Daughters of the State*, published by Bottlecap Press in 2021.

"I Still Like That Movie Where Nicolas Cage Plays Nicolas Cage" and "Chocolate Chip Pancakes" first appeared in *This Is How We Learn to Pray*, a poetry coloring book, illustrated by Stephanie Kirsten, and published by ELJ Editions, Ltd. in 2021.

Thank You

Thank you to my family for being my family. Thank you to Alan for giving these words a home. Thank you to Angelo for giving this book such a beautiful cover. Thank you to Zoë for telling everyone to read my book. Thank you to Adrienne for teaching me about commas and for making these poems look like poems. Thank you to Andrew and Travis and Adam and Ben and Ariana and Lauren and Mitchell and Nicole and the crew at *Olney Magazine* for your constant support and generosity. Thank you to the editors who said yes. Thank you to the editors who said no, but please try us again. Thank you to everyone I accidentally forgot to thank. Thank you to Leigh Chadwick. Thank you to _____ (name of Twitter follower) for putting up with my bullshit. Thank you to Jimmy Butler. Thank you to everyone who told me my poems mattered.

And thank you, dear reader, for choosing to spend your time with my words. I hope it's something you'll want to do again.

About the Author

Leigh Chadwick is the author of the chapbook *Daughters of the State*, the poetry coloring book *This Is How We Learn to Pray*, illustrated by Stephanie Kirsten, and the collaborative poetry collection *Too Much Tongue*, co-written with Adrienne Marie Barrios. Her poetry has appeared in *Salamander*, *Passages North*, *Pithead Chapel*, *The Indianapolis Review*, and *Hobart*. She is a regular contributor for *Olney Magazine*, where she conducts the "Mediocre Conversations" interview series.

Leigh can be found online at www.leighchadwick.com.

Encore! Encore! Encore!

Take a Femur, Leave a Femur

I decide to build a county fair in my back yard, so I go to Lowe's and buy a hammer, some nails, and a plastic children's pool for the dunk tank. On my way home from Lowe's, I steal some trees I find planted in a median in the middle of Johnson Street. When I get home, I chop up the trees and use the wood to build a seesaw.

I hire a Fat Elvis impersonator. Fat Elvis's job consists of sitting on one end of the seesaw and flinging the children who sit across from him into space. I hire a guy to do nothing but howl at the sky. He asks if he can whistle at any clouds shaped like the mole on Marilyn Monroe's cheek. I tell him, *Sure, have at it.*

A couple hours before we're set to open, Fat Elvis tells me he has to take a piss. Something to do with his prostate. I forgot to rent a Porta Potty and I've always kept a sparse yard, so there are no bushes for Fat Elvis or any of the future patrons to hide behind to take a piss. I decide I have no choice but to break into a nursing home and steal a closet full of catheters.

Even though it's daylight, I dress in all black and crawl through a window of the Sunny Meadows nursing home. I can't find a closet full of spare catheters, so I have to pull them out of the old folks trapped in the old folks' home.

I give fake Fat Elvis a catheter and then begin gluing toy ponies to a scratched Neutral Milk Hotel record. I am making a miniature merry-go-round where every guest can put a picture of what has left them on a pony and watch it go in circles. There is a sign in front of the merry-go-round stating everyone is expected to feel something. I put In the *Aeroplane Over the Sea* on the turntable, gently gliding the needle onto the record as the ponies spin in circles and the songs hiss and skip and eventually blur into a sound I haven't invented yet.

Entrance to the fair costs three Craigslist Missed Connections. A therapist stands at the exit of the hall of mirrors. She hands out her business card to everyone passing through. Most of them are crying.

By noon, we're out of elephant ears because I never made any to begin with. I raise my voice to drown out the guy I hired to howl at the sky and announce that a raffle will be held exactly thirty-seven minutes before dusk. Everyone who loves the color turquoise is able to participate. The winner will have to build Ikea furniture for the rest of the fiscal year.

My neighbor Phil trips over an abandoned catheter and falls on his face. Phil's nose is broken, twisted like a U-turn. His chin and neck painted pieces of sunset. No one helps Phil up off the ground because no one likes Phil.

The guy I hired to howl at the moon says he needs to take a break. He says his throat feels like it's coated in rust. His catheter bag is full and needs to be changed.

I ask him if he fell in love with a cloud today and he says maybe. He leaves the fairgrounds, and I know I'll never see him again.

I forgot to fill the dunk tank with water, so every time someone is dunked a piece of them breaks. I get tired of driving each of the fair-goers to the hospital, so I buy a bucket of femurs off eBay. I place the bucket of femurs on the side of the dunk tank. I tape a sign to the front of the bucket. It reads TAKE A FEMUR, LEAVE A FEMUR.

Shortly before the raffle is about to start, the police show up. A noise complaint. They want to know if I have a permit. I tell them, *It's a solemn thought, never being bitten by a radioactive spider.* I tell them, *I never had to make a diorama in high school.*

The cops aren't buying it.

I try again. *My parents are still together. They still hold hands as they walk up and down the aisles at Kroger.* I tell them, *I haven't had a nightmare in years. I'm too well-adjusted, though I once kissed a boy who didn't like icing on his Pop-Tarts.*

No icing? The officers shake their heads. *Some people,* they say.

Yes, I say. *Some people.*

The Last Poet Writes the Last Poem Before the World Ends

I never invite my nightmares over for dinner, but they show up anyway. They come carrying boxed wine. They eat all the dessert. They lick their plates clean. Sometimes my nightmares are an entire season of mud, but sometimes they're nothing but empty clouds drowning in dusk. Regardless of their weather, the nightmares tell me the same thing. They tell me I will be the last poet who will write the last poem before the world ends. They tell me the last poem will be composed minutes before the world ends. They tell me that the last poem will be pretty good but not great, and that in the penultimate stanza I will write, *Here's 2020. Fuck the moon and fuck the birds. And here's 2021, too. And here's a monster sweating Axe Body Spray.* The nightmares tell me that after finishing the last poem, I will black out from drinking all the boxed wine they brought over the night before, and that, hours later, I will wake up covered in mud, my head throbbing, my mouth a sandstorm. They tell me I will consider grabbing a couple of Tylenol from the medicine cabinet, but it won't matter because minutes later I will be dead.

Flash Sale

The new fall collection at Gap Kids comes in the choice of cotton or Kevlar. During recess, the kids play duck, duck, gun. Down the street and a few miles over, past the bridge that hangs above the river that's named after a state that has no reason to exist, a fifth body bag in as many days is zipped shut. A hip shatters. A cheek stretches apart. Molars bleach in the sun. Families nothing but glass and veins and dirty laundry. Families nothing but a fistful of hyphenated hearts scattered along the sidewalk.

The Poem of Bloom

For the last minute or hour, I've cried flowers to bloom. I weather thoughts as to whether my dreams will learn to crawl, whether the faceless man with kind eyes and sandpaper fingers will whittle wood into a boat and take me out to sea, take me far enough away that when I sleep, I am perfectly split between two continents. I imagine what follows hands reaching. I imagine being slit open. In my head, everything is bees. I wonder if I'm in heaven or hell. I wonder what the difference would be.

Sometimes I Dream in Centuries

I get a second job handing out tissues to willows. I trim my origami wings that are folded into swans. I floss the dandelions that sprout between my teeth. Outside my bedroom window, a rangale of deer graze in the lawn. The deer never stay for very long. It's as if they're always late to something. I wonder where deer go when they have somewhere to go. I wonder who invented the match, and who broke sound, and when will God get tired of carrying us around in his back pocket? If my house burned down, I would no longer have a house. I wish the deer knew I was thinking about them. I wish they would stay just a tiny bit longer.

About the Author, Pt. 2

Leigh Chadwick is based on a true story. Leigh Chadwick is the first day of sweater weather. Leigh Chadwick is your mother's mother. Leigh Chadwick drips from the hips. Leigh Chadwick is an interview with Leigh Chadwick where the first question of the interview is *Who is Leigh Chadwick?* Leigh Chadwick is not Sally Rooney but maybe one day. Leigh Chadwick is a parental advisory sticker on top of a parental advisory sticker. Leigh Chadwick is the fuck that made you realize how to fuck. Leigh Chadwick is a Franz Ferdinand guitar riff. Leigh Chadwick wakes up lightning. Leigh Chadwick was going to publish an excerpt of *Your Favorite Poet* in *The New Yorker* but decided she might fuck around and get rich and buy *The New Yorker* instead. Leigh Chadwick is not Banksy, though Banksy wishes Leigh Chadwick was Banksy. Leigh Chadwick is the last clove cigarette. Leigh Chadwick is Leigh Chadwick is Leigh Chadwick. Leigh Chadwick is soon to be a major motion picture.

Coming in May 2023

Sophomore Slump

Poems by

Leigh Chadwick

Other Malarkey Books Titles

The Life of the Party Is Harder to Find Until You're the Last One Around, Adrian Sobol
Forest of Borders, Nicholas Grider
Teacher Voice,
edited by Alan Good and DeMisty D. Bellinger
King Ludd's Rag,
a zine series featuring long short stories
Faith, Itoro Bassey
Music Is Over!, Ben Arzate
Toadstones, Eric Williams
It Came from the Swamp, edited by Joey R. Poole
Deliver Thy Pigs, Joey Hedger
Guess What's Different, Susan Triemert
White People on Vacation, Alex Miller
Man in a Cage, Patrick Nevins
Pontoon: volume 1, edited by Alan Good
Don Bronco's (Working Title) Shell, Donald Ryan
Fearless, Benjamin Warner
Thunder from a Clear Blue Sky, Justin Bryant
Un-ruined, Roger Vaillaincourt

malarkeybooks.com

Lightning Source UK Ltd.
Milton Keynes UK
UKHW010816010922
408173UK00003B/501